THE
UNNATURAL
LAW OF CELIBACY

THE UNNATURAL LAW OF CELIBACY

ONE MARRIED MAN'S STRUGGLE

TO BECOME A

ROMAN CATHOLIC PRIEST

RONALD N. EBERLEY

Continuum

NEW YORK • LONDON

2002

The Continuum International Publishing Group Inc
370 Lexington Avenue, New York, NY 10017

The Continuum International Publishing Group Ltd
The Tower Building, 11 York Road, London SE1 7NX

Copyright © 2002 by Ronald N. Eberley

All rights reserved. No part of this book may be reproduced, stored in a retrieval system, or transmitted in any form or by any means, electronic, mechanical, photocopying, recording or otherwise, without the written permission of the publishers.

Printed in the United States of America

Library of Congress Cataloging-in-Publication Data

Eberley, Ronald N.
The unnatural law of celibacy : one married man's struggle to become a Roman Catholic priest / Ron Eberley.
p. cm.
Includes bibliographical references and index.
ISBN 0-8264-1445-1 (hardcover)
1. Celibacy—Catholic Church. 2. Catholic Church—Clergy. 3. Eberley, Ron. I. Title.
BX1912.85 .E24 2002
253'.252—dc21
2002009765

CONTENTS

Foreword I by George A. Maloney, S.J.   7
Foreword II by Armand M. Nigro, S.J.   9
Introduction   13
1. My Childhood   19
2. Before Celibacy Was Obligatory   25
3. My Adolescence   39
4. Celibacy Becomes Mandatory for Ordination   47
5. My First Career   53
6. The Priesthood That I Knew   67
7. Marriage and Family   73
8. Official Changes Made to the Priesthood   87
9. My Second Career   91
10. The Ordained Priesthood in Crises   101
11. My Call to Priesthood   121
12. Contemporary Priesthood: A Different Job Description   137
13. On the Right Track   147

14. The Call Questioned: Why Celibate? Why Mandatory?   169
15. A Sequel   181
Acknowledgments   195
Bibliography   197
Notes   201

FOREWORD I

Ron Eberley has written a very important work concerning enforced celibacy for candidates to the priesthood in the Roman Catholic Church. He writes an individual historical narration that includes his early childhood, his desire to be a priest, his marriage and children, the death of his wife, his enrollment in a Catholic seminary for belated candidates for the priesthood, remarriage, and his petitioning bishops for permission to be ordained as a married priest. He intersperses and skillfully presents individual chapters of the history of the writings and actions of the Vatican, and the final enforcing of celibacy as a condition for ordination in the Latin church.

His excellent development of the historical accounts had me experiencing with Ron his suffering and that of thousands of excellent men in the church, who are still suffering in their long-held desire to be a "validly" ordained married priest. I have found from my personal experiences that priests in the various Eastern rites of the Catholic Church who were married were very much loved by their parishioners and were very prayerful priests.

I was ordained as a Jesuit of the Russian Catholic Rite in the hope of one day being missioned in Russia. My Jesuit formation training consisted of eighteen years of intensive prayer and studies, at the end of which I made my final profession of the vows of poverty, chastity, and obedience. I freely embraced God's gift of celibacy, not as a condition to be ordained but as a public witness of universal service in this gifted way. Never have I considered myself superior to Christian men who sought to serve God and the church as married Christians.

This is a most timely book that provides in-depth research on the history of the enforcement of celibacy, the shortage of priestly vocations throughout the entire world, and the importance of the gifts that married priests can bring to help the faithful in a sex-ridden society. Enforced celibacy is not a law from God. It is a Vatican law.

George A. Maloney, S.J.

FOREWORD II

This book is written for Catholics, with a special plea to its church leaders. The simple reform it espouses would benefit the entire world.

Ron Eberley's story, which I have urged him to publish, is the dilemma of thousands of Catholic married men who experience God calling them to priestly ministry. They are denied this privilege because they are married. What does this seem to say about our attitude toward sacramental married love?

The disciplinary ruling that all priests be celibate men has given us many saintly priests but has also deprived the church of many more good and saintly priests. That ruling can and should be easily and quickly dropped for diocesan priests.

We minority of priests in religious communities willingly make a vow of celibate chastity, because we are convinced God is calling us to religious life and we gratefully accept the gift of celibacy as essential to that life.

Unfortunately, celibacy has also been imposed on all diocesan priests not called to religious life, many of whom would have preferred to be married priests. Unfortunate? Yes, because we have always needed both married and celibate priests, and because we see the call to priesthood and the call to celibacy in the church as two distinct vocations.

The apostles of Jesus, says St. Paul in 1 Corinthians 9:5, were married, and the preferred choices of their successors, both bishops and priests, were faithfully married men who had reared good families (1 Tim 3:1–7 and Titus 1:5–9).

The Catholic Church has always had married priests in its Eastern rites. Presently, it wisely mitigates its requirement of celibacy and welcomes into its priesthood Episcopal and Protestant pastors desiring full union with the church, while remaining married and continuing their pastoral ministry. That same privilege is denied to married men who have been faithful Catholics all their lives. Does that discrimination make any sense?

The rapidly aging and diminishing number of priests in relation to the growing number of Catholics is a disaster in progress, because our people are being denied what they need and deserve: ready and regular access to the Eucharist, to the other sacraments, and to priestly ministry.

The solution, however, is very evident; it is readily available and the right thing to do: Without ceasing to nourish celibate priestly vocations, the entire church needs to recognize again and honor God's call of married men to priesthood, especially those who have raised good families and are ready for second careers. These men, like Ron Eberley, with the strong support of their wives, are living proofs that there has never been, nor is now, nor ever will be a lack of good priestly vocations in the church. God indeed is calling them.

It is a lack of faith to think the Holy Spirit does not provide all the various vocations and charisms (gifts for service) needed in every local church. It would seem to be an even greater lack of faith not to recognize and honor publicly the various vocations and charisms God does provide for our church, in both men and women, married or single, young or old (yes, and lay or clerical or religious) as indicated in St. Peter's first discourse (Acts 2) and as St. Paul affirms (1 Cor 12). Among the baptized there is no advantage to being either "Jew or Gentile, slave or free, male or female, for all are one in [the risen] Christ Jesus" (Gal 3:26–28). The Holy Spirit breathes wherever and empowers whomever He wills (John 3:8).

Married candidates, with the cooperation of their wives, can easily be prepared in the dioceses where they live, just as deacons and their wives have been. We need them and can no longer do without them.

The present seminary system since the Council of Trent has produced many great priests and theologians, but largely it is a failed system because of its nearly exclusive focus on boys and younger men. Less than twenty percent (probably less than fifteen percent if an accurate accounting were made of the last one hundred years) of all who entered any seminary were ordained and persevered to death as faithful priests. If similar statistics were true of professional schools, most people would recognize those educational systems as failures and a misuse of resources.

After over forty years of service in seminaries and formation programs of men and women around the world, I am aware that most of our energy and time and expense was expended to help immature youngsters become responsible adults, before we entrusted them with pastoral ministry.

Instead of fishing for priestly vocations primarily out of the same drying-up water holes of young people, at great expense and with diminishing returns, it is time to recognize that good married Catholics are the large fertile bonanza of better priestly recruits, because they are already mature, wiser, more experienced, reliable, of more solid virtue, and have proven track records. What you see and find there you get. Not the roll of the dice we now have with younger men, who have rarely made a living or been responsible for the maintenance and well being of a family or of any others—and who are not all that certain of their call to life-long celibacy.

The Ministry Institute of Mater Dei, in conjunction with our Jesuit Gonzaga University in Spokane, Washington, has prepared seventy men for priesthood (averaging over fifty years of age) since 1982, and a growing number of women and men for lay pastoral ministry.* They now serve the church across the United States and Canada, and on six continents. Ron Eberley was one of our best seminarians. Very few failed to complete their programs and not a single one, approved by its staff for ordination, has either left the priesthood or shamed the church. Is there any other seminary in the world that can say that?

Mater Dei has developed into a ministry training institute for both men and women, including married couples, discerning their calls to ministry, while pursuing ministry degrees. Priests and sisters from the developing world come there as well, to prepare for service in seminaries and religious formation in their own countries. Other adults enjoy spiritual sabbaticals there.

The primary reason for Mater Dei's success, besides God's lavish

---

*Mater Dei Institute, 405 E. Sinto, Spokane, WA, 99201. Telephone 1-800-986-9585, Ext. 6037.

grace, is the maturity of the students accepted, most of whom have raised good families. The formula is a winner.

With the Catholic birthrate dramatically down (about two children per marriage), far fewer priestly and religious vocations are being nurtured. Parents want grandchildren and are not happy at the prospect of their only son or daughter becoming a celibate priest or religious sister. There are, however, plenty of men like Ron desiring to respond to a God-given call to priesthood.

Our disastrous spiral, then, of fewer priests for growing numbers of practicing Catholics would be solved. And far from harming those marriages, the priesthood should powerfully grace and enhance the beauty and strength of their sacramental marriages and their families.

The purpose of Ron Eberley's book, and of this foreword, is to spark fruitful discussions and especially prayer and a groundswell of concerned Catholics to beg our Catholic leaders to heed the Holy Spirit and to give us soon the married as well as celibate diocesan priests we need.

Armand M. Nigro, S.J.

INTRODUCTION

> When it is evening, you say, 'It will be fair weather, for the sky is red.' And in the morning, 'It will be stormy today, for the sky is red and threatening.' You know how to interpret the appearance of the sky, but you cannot interpret the signs of the times.
>
> Matthew 16:3

There is provision in the canon law of the Catholic Church to grant a dispensation for a man to receive the sacrament of orders "because he has a wife," as canon 1047 states. But the avenues of communication for anyone seeking this dispensation are closed. The critical shortage of priests continues to worsen. Leaders in the church are not interpreting "the signs of the times" crying out for change. At a training session for nonordained ecclesial ministers learning to preside at Communion services for "priestless Sundays," one of the trainees likened the priest shortage to our standing on a railway track with a train bearing down on us, while nobody seems to care!

I write this book as the means to influence the church of my heritage. I have exhausted all of the usual and reasonable means to communicate with episcopal administrators in the church. I have concluded that bishops are under restrictions, which limit their freedom to act. I believe this sincerely, because most of the bishops whom I contacted are good and reasonable men, who by their responses seemed constrained from doing what they wanted to do.

My adult life in the church prior to becoming a professional ecclesial minister was always to be supportive of priests and to witness to the faith of the church. I did so while I was a member of the Royal Canadian Mounted Police (RCMP), frequently attending worship services in uniform out of necessity, almost always serving in smaller municipalities and therefore known to be a Catholic Christian policeman. While I was single, my service in the police force resulted in transfers every year. After I was married, my family and I were transferred virtually every three years. I lived and was active in more than a dozen different Catholic parishes in western Canada from 1955 through 1987.

I left the RCMP in 1976 as a consequence of a number of events and much recourse to prayer. After brief experiences with outside sales, I became the manager of an industry association for two and a half years and for another nine years was employed with one of the association's member companies in residential land development. This second career was built upon my skills and experience as a planner that had been learned in the police force. I continued to be active in Catholic parishes. My activities were primarily in liturgical music but included membership in pastoral councils and in liturgical planning groups. My support of priests in various parishes included both diocesan and order priests—notably Oblates of Mary Immaculate, Basilians, Franciscans, and Redemptorists.

During my third career as a professional ecclesial minister, I felt inhibited from writing this book because it would be open for the public to evaluate and seemingly would be airing laundry in public. I continued to confront and was confronted by issues of injustice within the institutional church. The Catholic Church is a very public church. Over the centuries its leaders have not always acted in the best interests of the people of God. There are many indications that the best interests of the people of God are again being sidestepped. I have witnessed numerous facts and events that are clear "signs of the times" calling for the elimination of mandatory celibacy for diocesan priests in the Western church. From this experience and out of love for the church and for the priesthood, I have no alternative but to present my autobiography and its attendant observations, to influence the church from the grassroots level, to look at this problem objectively.

This book is written to record numerous signs of the times available to the people of God for guidance and even as requisite evidence to support certain acts of faith. In biblical thought, "the basic meaning of [a] sign is [a] symbol which indicates the existence or the presence of that which it signifies; it directs the attention to the reality signified."[1] Such signs may manifest patterns or repetitions of life experience, from which we may derive meaning and understanding in faith. "Men and women are always called to direct their steps towards a truth which transcends them."[2]

Sometimes there can be difficulty in reading the signs of the times on behalf of the people of God. All manner of things can get in the way. This book is about signs of the times that connect the church's historic approach to human sexuality and the crisis of its diminishing priesthood. This book includes my personal story when connecting those signs of the times. Integrated with this autobiographical account are many signs of the times I came to see through questioning, research, experience, and working full time in the church as a nonordained ecclesial minister. They are presented in relation to my life's story because my experience is part of the global signs of the times, namely, the critical shortage of priests in the universal church, which church leaders seem unable or unwilling to "interpret" properly.

As with all decisions made in our historic church, it is important that we understand the context within which earlier decisions were made. We cannot judge the rationality and appropriateness of earlier decisions from contemporary perspectives, which have the benefit of present knowledge and insights not available to church leaders long ago.

Whenever I raise issues and challenge traditions in this book, I do so in a spirit of renewal, which is always essential to the church, which exists to perpetuate the mission of Jesus Christ. I am certain that Jesus Christ, who never wrote a book, was well aware that members of his church would "mess things up" from time to time. We don't have far to go to substantiate this certitude. Among the apostles whom Jesus chose, we know that one sold him out, another denied him, and all twelve fled from Gethsemane, leaving him alone to face his trials and death.

Characteristic of our historic church is its authoritarian rule which for the most part has remained dominant over the people of God. The church in the Western hemisphere has been well described as a church in which the people of God were called upon to "pay, pray, and obey." Something very major happened that changed that. The major happening was the Second Vatican Council (1962 to 1965) initiating the greatest change in the Catholic Church in four hundred years. There were immediate effects, of course, but the more comprehensive and profound changes are still occurring. Unfortunately, codependency to centuries of institutional authoritarianism has seriously stalled a more timely and valuable corrective. As a result, many Catholics continue in the former mindset. Eighteen years elapsed before the revised Code of Canon Law was promulgated in 1983. This updated law of the church extended to the faithful certain rights, one of which is the right to make one's opinions known to the pastors of the church (canon 212 §3). If the faithful have that right, then the pastors have a duty to listen. I have written this book because the pastors of the church are demonstrably unable or unwilling to listen. My intention in this writing is not to establish blame for their failure to listen but to influence the cause.

Many Catholic leaders and laity continue their lives in the church in the "pay, pray, and obey" mentality, with the notion that we ought not to question. My life experience and the experience of many people of my generation in the church confirm the existence of that attitude. Because this obedient, accepting, nonquestioning attitude continues to be held at least by some of the people of God in every parish and diocese, I will offer justification for the things I raise throughout the book. People do not make a one hundred and eighty degree change just because a new canon is promulgated. What had been their way of life will only give way gradually. Neither do pastors make one hundred and eighty degree changes quickly. In the postconciliar period, church leaders have frequently been heard to "remind" God's people that the Catholic Church is not a democracy. The notion is that having a vote in the church is different from having a say, but the people of God have a rightful say and thus the church ought to function more democratically if people are to experience this "right."

The very slow pace of some changes has to do with our being creatures of habit who dislike change. This is remarkable because the only constant in life *is* change! When I became an instructor of management practices in the police force, I learned that while people resist change, they readily change when they understand the reasons for it. It is not so much what happens to us but what we do about it that is critical and how we handle the changes in our lives. This book is intended to assist our church leaders in handling the change that is upon us. Lest this seem presumptuous, I make some claim to leadership, having served in the church professionally for the past eight years, albeit in a parish community. An affirmation supporting my claim occurred when our parish organist introduced me to two members of his family as a deacon. When I clarified that I was nonordained, the organist responded, "Well, you are one of the 'mucky-mucks' around here!"

I decided to write my autobiography as a silhouette against the backdrop of the history of celibacy in the Catholic Church, a juxtaposition—one miniscule life against centuries of Catholic Christian tradition. Beginning with my childhood, I alternate successive chapters of my life with the history of celibacy, the time lines of which are not God's measurements but ours. I feel impelled to publish this writing after much prayer and discernment, so that the people of God and especially the bishops of the church may objectively reassess *obligatory* celibacy for diocesan priests and observe *authentic* subsidiarity and acknowledge the *sin* of sexism. If only a parish "mucky-muck," I present this work with some credibility, because the events of these related histories are about the pursuit of truth and justice, which is God's measurement.

1

MY CHILDHOOD

> When I was a child, I spoke like a child, I thought like a child, I reasoned like a child.
> 1 Corinthians 13:11

I was born the second of five boys to Frank and Agnes Eberley on August 25, 1935, in the Misericordia Hospital in Winnipeg, Manitoba. I was baptized in the "Belgian Church," properly known as Sacred Heart Church, in St. Boniface, on September 8, 1935. This is significant to me because September 8 is the day on which we celebrate the birth of Mary, the mother of Jesus. My mother was Belgian, from a large family, and was fluent in French, English, and Flemish. Mother was a good woman, solid in her faith, and quite "persnickety" in her approach to raising five boys. Dad and Mom supported each other and we were all quite afraid to incur Dad's displeasure.

I went to kindergarten at Maison Chapelle in St. Boniface when I was five years old. I received my initial religious training from the French nuns who managed to instill a certain fear in me about the things of God—especially about offending God! I was confirmed that year by Archbishop Cabana who tapped me on the cheek, as was the practice then, signifying the strength required to be a "soldier for Christ."

My cousin George and I were quite close during childhood. We both attended Provencher School, an all-boys' school, from grade one through twelve. It was named after Bishop Provencher and was run by the Brothers of Mary. I was taught in grade one by a laywoman, then completed grades two and three in one year under Miss Bonin and accelerated to grade four in Miss Marion's class. Either Miss Marion did not think I should be in grade four or she was just very very strict. Finally, in grade five I was taught by one of the brothers. I always remember him—Brother Beaulieu, a pipe-smoking, wonderful man. He told us that when we went to bed at night, if all we said was "Lord your mule is tired," that would be sufficient prayer!

Mother's side of the family was dominant, holding large family gatherings at Christmas and other special occasions. George's Dad, Joseph, was mayor of St. Boniface and my godfather. On one occasion when I was walking by the city hall I saw George, who was quite well dressed, accompanying his Dad to some official function. I was dressed in play clothes, with muddy shoes, but managed to stand with George for a while, a little to the chagrin of my uncle. He and his brother, my uncle Frank, owned and operated a hotel in St. Boniface for many years. There was a large extended family on Mother's side.

My Dad's side of the family was smaller. They were of the Lutheran tradition and lived in Winnipeg proper. We lived in St. Boniface, which in later years became part of greater Winnipeg under a centralized government. I barely remember my paternal grandfather, but I have fond memories of sitting on Grandma Eberley's lap and listening to her stories. When she died, I saw her in her open casket at a funeral home in Winnipeg. I was being held by my Dad and I reached down to open her eyelid as I was sure Grandma was just sleeping. Dad took my hand away and I guess I knew then—she wasn't sleeping. I was about three years old at the time.

It is remarkable to remember early events of life quite clearly. Another such event was the 1939 visit of King George and Queen Elizabeth to St. Boniface. I went with my Dad and there were many people standing on the sidewalk along the route where the open convertible car was to pass. Dad sat me on his shoulders and I had a good view of the car and its illustrious passengers as it drove by. I was four years old!

For the most part my early childhood in St. Boniface was quite happy. My oldest brother, Bernie, and I began serving mass at the cathedral in St. Boniface. We were in the English-speaking "triangle." There were twelve triangles—identified by twelve closets or armoires, in which hung ten cassocks, surplices, and birettas, one for each altar boy. Eleven of the triangles were French speaking. Actually, Bernie and I could speak broken French and even had a French accent as a result of playing in our St. Boniface neighborhood. I know that it was a little too much French for my Dad. He became a Catholic when he married Mother but stopped going to church after a while. He evidently didn't want Bernie and me to serve mass at the cathedral, but Mother and he argued about it and Mother stuck to her guns and so off we went. Most of the time when I went to church until I was ten years old it was at the cathedral where the sermons were always in French.

When I was still a young altar boy at St. Boniface Cathedral, Cardinal Villeneuve came from Montreal. I was a trainbearer and had to wear white gloves to hold his train, which was a ten-foot-long attachment to his scarlet cassock. There was much pomp and ceremony and I was part of it. There were hikes and outings for altar boys and these formed part of our socializing. I learned to ice skate first on bob skates then on tube skates. I used to watch the priests play hockey on the outdoor ice at St. Boniface College. They would tie up their cassocks around their waists so they wouldn't get in the way. These were usually pick-up games for fun. My younger brother next to me was Chuck and next to him was Bill. Sometimes Chuck would be with Bernie and me but not very much at St. Boniface, because Chuck and Bill were quite young at the time.

Bernie and I frequently played "saying mass" on the dining room table, taking turns as to who would be the altar boy and who would be the priest. We had to learn Latin responses in those days, and if anything the French accent helped us with the Latin pronunciation. Once or twice I accompanied Dad in his truck with King's Old Country Beverages. On one occasion we drove into the country in pouring rain across the flat terrain and graveled roads of the grain-farming area around Winnipeg. I was quite afraid of the thunder, especially when we stopped at a country store and Dad got out of the truck and I was alone in the cab. At most I was six or seven years old.

During the same age period, I accompanied Dad to the shore of the Red River a mile or so from our house. Dad had a green fishing line to which he tied a couple of bolts for weight and a hook, baited with an earthworm, which I watched him find in our garden before we left. He swung a yard or two of the end of the baited and weighted fishing line in a large circle several times over his head until it had gained sufficient momentum to let it go toward the center of the river. He tied the line to a willow branch that he inserted perpendicularly into the ground. We then sat down and watched the branch. When it jerked wildly we knew we had caught a fish and I watched Dad pull the line into a neat pile at his feet. Usually he caught catfish, which I thought were quite ugly with large whiskers that could stick you if you weren't careful while taking the fish off the hook. Sometimes Dad would have two fishing lines in the water and we watched two willow branches. Usually we caught five or six fish in a couple of hours or so, and on the way home Dad would stop at a small shack near the river and give the fish to an old man who lived there.

I learned to ride a bicycle in St. Boniface on my Dad's double crossbar two-wheeler, from which I managed to fall several times. I know this was when I was eight or nine years old, because by that time Dad was working for the Canadian National Railway and he had to use the bicycle to ride to work. We did not own a car at the time. Dad always encouraged my brother and me to learn to ride the bike. Soon there was talk at home of moving to Kamloops, British Columbia. This went on for some months, while Mom and Dad negotiated selling the house and Dad arranged for a transfer with the railway to Kamloops. My mother's aunt and uncle, Alice and Bill, lived in Kamloops. Mom thought that would be a better place for us to live, and perhaps Dad would come to church more often where the sermon wouldn't always be in French. We looked forward to the move and to the idea of attending St. Anne's Academy there, which was a coed school. I had never gone to school with girls in the class and the idea seemed inviting.

When I was nine years old, Mom and Dad took Bernie and me to the Belgian Club and got us started playing in the band there. We had already been taking piano lessons for about a year. I learned how to play the trombone and Bernie the euphonium. I didn't have much skill on the instrument, but we used to practice in the band once a week. Mr. Mitchell, the conductor, was very supportive. Bernie and I marched with the band down the streets of Winnipeg on one occasion. I was in the front row where the trombones normally marched. We must have looked cute, a nine and eleven year old mixed in with adult bandsmen!

On "firecracker" day, Queen Victoria's birthday, May 24 about 1942, our house caught fire. We lived in a two-story house on Notre Dame Street. A couple rented the upstairs and had evidently left a pot of oil on a burner while they walked to the corner store. Dad heard something popping upstairs and went up to check. I was standing at the bottom of the stairs when I heard a loud thud and then saw the whole staircase burst into flames. Dad came running down the stairs through the flames and told me to get outside. The telephone was at the foot of the stairs and Dad called the fire department and got us all out of the house. I learned later that Dad had taken the boiling oil off the stove and slipped on the waxed floor, and when he fell the oil hit the wooden staircase and burst into flames. Dad sat with us on the front porch that evening with his hands and feet bandaged. He was many weeks recovering from the burns he received.

Occasionally I went to evening devotions at the Convent of the Sisters of the Precious Blood with my mother. It was an occasion when prayers were recited in conjunction with Benediction of the Blessed Sacrament. I would kneel beside her, not really knowing what was going on, but when I looked up I saw her with her eyes closed in prayer. Coupled with all the little teachings and explanations Mom gave me, this image of her at prayer never left me. We are real imitators in our learning and that image was both a manifestation of faith and an example to me, which I picked up and have carried ever since.

I had been old enough to read the newspaper while in St. Boniface. I used to see pictures of Canadian servicemen who were killed or missing in action. By hearing things from adults about the war and from the little I read, I knew it was awful. I would look out the window and hear the train switching boxcars. When I heard loud bangs of rail cars being connected, I imagined this was the sound of cannons. I was afraid the war was coming closer. Beyond these childhood fears I wasn't directly affected.

Finally the day came when we moved to Kamloops. We traveled by train on Dad's pass. It was a two-and-a-half day trip and I slept in an upper berth. We arrived in Kamloops on August 15, 1945. People were dancing in the street because it was the end of World War II. For our family it was a double celebration. It took a while for Dad to gain possession of the house he had purchased, and we stayed in the hotel that my mother's aunt and uncle owned. Soon after our arrival in Kamloops, my mother heard about a band and an orchestra starting up. Mother went to see the director and soon we were able to continue playing our instruments in that band.

I began grade six at Lloyd George School, one of several public elementary schools in Kamloops, because St. Anne's had been demolished by an arson fire and was being totally rebuilt. The public school system had agreed to take in one class per school. I am sure it was more difficult for the sisters and other teachers who had to accommodate us, but for the students like myself it was just fine. Kamloops had a population of ten thousand when we moved there. Dad bought us each a used bicycle, and Bernie and I took on paper routes delivering an advertising flyer twice a week. Later we each acquired a daily morning newspaper route which was a little more demanding and of course a little more profitable. Mother frequently sent me to the grocery store with ration books, and whenever I was able to buy sugar or some other commodity that had been rationed due to the war, it was quite exciting for me to come home and tell Mom so she could make a fuss over my shopping skills.

2

BEFORE CELIBACY WAS OBLIGATORY

> Then Moses came down from the mountain to the people and had them sanctify themselves and wash their garments. He warned them, "Be ready for the third day. Have no intercourse with any woman."
>
> Exodus 19: 14–15

The childhood of my life was a long time ago. So, too, relatively speaking, was the infancy of Christianity. It may seem surreal to equate one human life with the "life" of Christianity, but a certain relevance comes to mind. As St. Paul says, "When I was a child I spoke, thought, and reasoned like a child." The "childhood" of Christianity was a time of experimenting, learning, and growing. It emerged from the life and ministry of Jesus, who was born totally dependent and vulnerable, and matured to adulthood in Roman-occupied Palestine of late antiquity. Jesus preached the coming of God's reign and revealed that all human beings are loved unconditionally by the God of love. He confronted practices that held to the letter of the law and espoused keeping "the spirit of the law" instead. He took a stand for truth and justice and in so doing gave his life for God's people. He rose from the dead, and Christianity was born. It did not begin with a celibate priesthood.

Most of the Apostles were married. Scripture records that Jesus cured Peter's mother-in-law (Mk 1:29–31; Mt 8:14–15; Lk 4:38–39). Paul wrote: "Do we not have the right to be accompanied by a believing wife as do the rest of the Apostles and brothers of the Lord and Cephas?" (1 Cor 9:5) He continued: "Nevertheless, we have not made use of this right, but we endure anything rather than put an obstacle in the way of the gospel of Christ" (1 Cor 9:12). Paul does not argue for compulsory celibacy for anyone else, even while he favors celibacy for itinerant Christian missionaries: "But I have made no use of any of these rights, nor am I writing this so that they may be applied in my case" (1 Cor 9:15).

Leaders in the infant church struggled to integrate the teachings of Jesus and the preaching of the earliest evangelists into the worldview and social world they inhabited. Marking that infancy were conflicts between certain religious truths and values and existing notions of human sexual experience. Primitive understandings of human sexuality and procreation characterized and inhibited this early evolutionary journey, much as occurs when children come to the awareness of sexuality.

There were sexual taboos in the Hebrew Scriptures. Candidates for priesthood were required to abstain sexually for seven days to be ritually pure (Lev 8:33), and for three days this priestly regulation was extended to all the people, symbolic of the period of waiting for the law at Sinai (Ex 19:15). However, few of these cultic observances in relation to the sexual act were carried into the New Testament. Instead, the old cultic institutions and personnel were suspended.[1]

The introduction of Christianity in areas dominated by Jewish and pagan traditions raised complex issues. The Jewish practice of circumcision was not required of the Gentile converts by St. Paul. This was upsetting to some of the Jewish converts to Christianity to the extent that it was discussed at the Council of Jerusalem (Acts 15:1–29 and Gal 2:1–10). Paul experienced agitation from those who insisted upon circumcision so much so that he wrote to the Galatians: "Would that those who are troubling you [about the law of circumcision] might go the whole way and castrate themselves" (Gal 5:12). Other conflicts arose that are recorded in Scripture, for instance, St. Paul's letter to Timothy requesting him to "stay in Ephesus to instruct certain people not to teach false doctrines or to concern themselves with myths and endless genealogies, which promote speculations rather than the plan of God that is to be received by faith" (1 Tim 1:3b–4). The infant church was leaving behind some of the former laws and rituals recorded in the Hebrew Scriptures. It was a time of learning, growing, and discovering the meaning of "I have not come to abolish [the law and the prophets] but to fulfill them" (Mt 5:17).

Among Roman upper classes adultery and fornication were very common. Among the Hebrews, sex was approved within marriage, not solely for procreation but for mutual pleasure and fulfillment as well. The Hebrews believed that the expression of sexual needs and desires helped to strengthen marriage and solidified the family. Early Christians tolerated sex in marriage but saw temptations of the flesh as distractions from spiritual devotion to God. They viewed marriage as inferior to celibacy and began to associate sexuality with sin.[2]

The life of citizens in the Roman Empire during the second century was marked by a life expectancy for young men of less than twenty-five years. Many died young and those that survived childhood remained at risk. About four men in one hundred and fewer women lived beyond the age of fifty. Begetting and rearing children to replace the dead was an expectation. It was sometimes spurred on by legislation as in the case of the emperor Augustus who penalized bachelors and rewarded families for producing children. Mere maintenance of the population required of each woman the production of an average of five children. Young girls were recruited early for their task such that the median marrying age of Roman girls was possibly as low as fourteen. Bachelors existed in upper-class circles despite their being urged to marry. Virgin women, too, had been part of the timeless religious landscape of the classical world. Early attitudes toward human sexuality included examples of permanent sexual renunciation—continence, celibacy, and life-long virginity. By around the year 150 renunciation of sexual expression had come to mean various things to different Christian groups.[3]

Males in the second century held a position of unchallenged dominance. Women, slaves, and barbarians were inferiors. It was held that biologically males were those fetuses that had realized their full potential. Women, on the other hand, were viewed as failed males. This made them more liquid, soft, clammy-cold, and more formless than men. Men feared becoming "womanish." They consciously strove to maintain their manhood and to remain "virile." This impacted their deportment and conduct in relation to their inferiors.[4] The hierarchical pattern of the family was such that the male was always superior to the female as surely as parents were to children and masters were to slaves. This pattern was deeply entrenched in the law and customs and any erosion of it was fiercely deplored.[5]

There were pagan virgin priestesses. The Vestal Virgins at Rome and the virgin priestesses and prophetesses of the classical Greek world were deemed crucially important for the community because they were anomalous. (These virgin women tended the temple fires as followers of Vesta, goddess of the hearth in Roman mythology, also identified as the Greek Hestia.) This pagan chastity was evidently not a matter of free choice for those women. They were recruited and dedicated to the service of the gods. Many virgin priestesses were free to marry later in life. The contrived suspension of the normal process for girls moving from puberty to childbearing rendered these virgins as exceptions that reinforced the rule. Vestal Virgins who didn't marry until they were thirty stood out as glaring anomalies. Their presence, chosen by others to forego marriage, increased the awareness that marriage and childbearing were unquestionably the destiny for all other women.[6]

Rigorous attitudes toward sexuality developed among some Christians culminating in a sect believed to have originated in Syria or Mesopotamia and referred to as Encratism (which means *abstinence*). Adherents held that women were a creation of the devil and men were halfway similarly created but above the waist were creatures of God. Thus the coupling of a man and woman in marriage was doubly the work of the devil. Many early church leaders opposed all forms of Encratism and other attitudes inimical to marriage. The rigidities of the Encratic sect included negative views of women, wine, and the eating of meat. About the year 170 a threat of schism (separation from orthodox Christianity) arose but was suppressed with the condemnation of Tatianus in 172. As these negative views persisted, it became clear that the main problem was not the connection between office in the church and celibacy but that between baptism and celibacy. This was a problem in the Syrian church as late as the third century, where chastity was called "the crown of baptism" and was practiced in that way. The bishop of Knossos named Dionysius reproached a fellow bishop for requiring "the heavy yoke of virginity to be laid upon the faithful." Ignatius, bishop of Antioch, wrote several letters that became well known in the early church. Polycarp, bishop of Smyrna, evidently disseminated these, one of which asked him not to demand celibacy of his Christians.[7]

Pagan critics viewed Christianity as a religion notorious for the close association between men and women—a group with secret signs whose members fall in "love" almost before they are acquainted. Pagans inferred promiscuity from the Christian notions of "brotherhood" and "sisterhood." By the year 200 various existing Christian groups had accused other Christian groups of bizarre sexual practices. A young man seeking to persuade pagans that indiscriminate intercourse was not what Christian men sought in their "sisters," petitioned the Augustal Prefect in the time of Justin for permission to be castrated. It seems that, aside from the slurs of pagans and fellow Christians and the spirit-filled heroism of the martyrs, surprisingly little is known about the relations of men and women in the Christian communities of the second and early third centuries.[8]

In addition to the threat of execution, other aspects of the pagan persecution of Christians consisted of attempts at sexual violence and threats of condemnation to brothels. Christian asceticism associated with some form of perpetual sexual renunciation was an established feature of most of the Christian world. The forms of renunciation varied greatly, carried a different message, and resulted in different patterns of life in the local churches. In the West, holiness of fleshly continence was the tendency among the clergy. Such clergymen had frequently been married and raised families, but to continue to have intercourse with their wives was increasingly regarded as shocking. Ultimately, two ways of life became common: one forgoing marriage and childbearing entirely; the other, a more humble, human way involving marriage, children, and occupational pursuits other than religion.[9]

There are three "priesthoods" relevant to our subject: pagan, Jewish, and Christian. The New Testament normally uses the words *priest* or *high priest* to refer to the Jewish Levitical priests (e.g., Mt 8:4) or to pagan priests (Acts 14:13). When applied to Christianity, the word *priest* or *high priest* is used only of Christ, as in Hebrews 5:6–8, or to all the faithful, as in Revelation 1:6 and 20:6. Reference to the pagan priesthood relates to the cultural world encountered by the gospel in its beginnings. The established pagan religions were essentially a cult of forces acting in nature, aimed at making them favorable by the performance of certain rites. It was a cult rather than a belief, a religion in which sacrificial rites were performed not out of piety or for spiritual communion but to pay a religious tax, as it were, in the name of the community or city. In antiquity acts of divination and oracles were included in the attributes of that priesthood. That cult existed to make people happy in this present life and the pagan gods were essentially personifications of the mysterious elements of nature, such as water, wind, sun, and fertility.[10]

The forgoing reference to Yves Congar's book *A Gospel Priesthood* is critical to our understanding of the origins of sexual repression in Christianity. Congar's writing about Christian priesthood emphasizes that the priest of the gospel is not a magician of some unseen world. From beginning to end the gospel has always meant substituting actions of faith for mere rites and things. Congar says Christians had instinctively replaced the hired mourners of pagan and even Jewish funerals, and musical instruments in the services, with the singing of psalms. More particularly, New Testament worship is worship "in spirit and in truth." The priests who preside in these celebrations are neither magicians nor even Levites of the Law of Moses.[11]

Certain apocryphal (or noncanonical) writings that emphasized continence claimed that salvation would be out of the question for married persons who continued to have conjugal relations. More dangerous were neo-Pythagorean sources, which spread the Hellenistic notion that sexual intercourse and prayer were contradictory, and thus castration was recommended. This was apparently literally applied by Egyptian monks and by Origen.[12]

Quiet revolutions determined the future development of religion in Europe and the Near East, namely, the rise to dominance of the rabbis within Judaism and the creation of a strict division between clergy and laity in the Christian church. Jews of high social status, who were wealthy married benefactors, supported the scholars and synagogues. The Christian churches were in a similar position. In the Great Church of Christianity, segregated from those groups branded as heretics, it became plain that the rank and file gained merit by providing support for the chosen few. They did this by offering the community the things that the elite had renounced: wealth and children. This was most telling as the infant church emerged amid the struggles concerning continent clergy and reproductive laity. Moreover, for Christianity there was the constant anxiety for its clergy to define their position against the principal benefactors of the Christian community. It came to be recognized that leaders should possess recognizable and perpetual tokens of superiority to the laity. They might be expected to give evidence of a charismatic calling and they were encouraged, if possible, to practice perpetual continence. Ultimately, they received ordination through the "laying on of hands." This gave the clergy an exclusive role in the celebration of the Eucharist, the central rite of the Christian community, and ensured that leadership would not gravitate to the wealthiest, most powerful benefactors.[13]

For most of the first twelve centuries of the church, both married and unmarried men were welcomed as ministers. Reasons why some remained unmarried were personal, social, or religious. In the early centuries of the church, ministry was increasingly compared with the priesthood of the Hebrew Scriptures. Laws of purity for pagan priests influenced the general cultural climate of antiquity in the areas of the Mediterranean; for example, anyone who approached the altar was not to have enjoyed the pleasures of Venus the night before. Neo-Platonic dualism played a part in the pessimistic view of sexuality. The early Christians were people of their age even though they were critical of their pagan surroundings. In the earliest Christian churches, sexual abstinence was regarded by some, as we have seen, as a baptismal obligation. The church defended marriage against such views as being holy and good and a gift from God at creation. However, pressure from the pagan environment led to the more reserved view that "the use of marriage" was only permissible for the purposes of procreation and any pleasure associated with it was not quite right. A more or less universally pessimistic view was held by pagans and Christians alike that, in the words of St. Jerome, "sexual intercourse is impure."[14]

The Christian teacher Origen (185–254 C.E.) presented virginity as a privileged link between heaven and earth. Since it was through the "holy" body of a virgin woman that God had joined Himself to humanity, human nature might become divine through prolonged relatedness with divinity. Perpetual continence was now upheld for a wide variety of reasons by little groups of Christian men and women throughout the Mediterranean. Origen felt such Christians clearly represented God's deepest purposes for the transformation of humanity. Christian communities had grown rapidly in the course of the third century. Families were encouraged not to marry their daughters to Jews, pagans, or heretics. Their daughters often opted for voluntary continence, and as such were protected and esteemed by the clergy. Even young men began opting for perpetual celibacy quite distinct from the postmarital continence that had prevailed earlier. Thus groups of radical men and women committed to the virginal state grew up within Christian communities.[15]

I have searched for the defining basis for sexual renunciation in early Christianity. It appears to have originated for two reasons:

1. A pre-Christian suggestion that remaining in virginity or the state of a eunuch brings one closer to God. (This was apparently intelligible to contemporary pagans and Jews, both of whom believed that abstinence from sexual activity, and especially virginity, rendered the human body more appropriate to receive divine inspiration.)

2. The strong emphasis on the virgin birth of Christ in the Gospel of Luke points to a mentality where virginity and the gift of prophecy were closely linked. (At times a man could be spoken of with esteem as a eunuch and virgin girls appeared to be prophets, but these were exceptions. It was more often the case that prophets entered their calling as elderly persons, having conceived children and having raised them as Christians.)[16]

Ostensibly the first regulation in relation to celibacy was contained in canon 33 of the Council of Elvira (306 C.E.). This council of bishops and priests of the Spanish church assembled in the diocese of Elvira near Granada. Canon 33 contained the following text: "It has seemed good absolutely to forbid the bishops, the priests, and the deacons, i.e., all the clerics engaged in service at the altar, to have [sexual] relations with their wives and procreate children; should anyone do so, let him be excluded from the honor of the clergy." The intent of this regulation was to restore legal unity and stability to the church in that region of Spain. This was apparently not a new law, but a reaction to *"the prevalent nonobservance"* of a traditional obligation that was well known. The effect of this canon was that the clergy were to observe the obligation they had undertaken or renounce the clerical office. The conclusion of some historians is that the majority of clergy at that time were men who married before they were ordained, but after having received sacred orders, they were obliged to renounce the further use of marriage and to observe complete continence.[17]

The monastery became an elite form of Christianity, especially after the legalization of Christianity under Constantine in 312 C.E. The chief reason for monastic celibacy was asceticism, and this was often based on a pessimistic dualism that was un-Christian. The ideal of the monastic community interacted with the clerical order that also emerged in the early centuries of the church. Thus the clerical order became drawn into the Christian elite, and this made the adoption of celibacy more or less inevitable, particularly where the clergy could practice some form of common life. The influence of figures like Jerome, Augustine, and Benedict resulted in widespread communal celibacy, though for many individual clerics marriage and the full use of marriage remained the rule.[18]

An authoritative stance that sought to impose sexual abstinence on the part of married clergy evolved. It developed gradually. In his treatise on the subject, Alfons Maria Cardinal Stickler points out: "It is a particular characteristic of law, explained in every history on the topic, that the origin of every legal system consists in oral traditions and in the transmission of customary norms which only slowly receive a fixed written form." He goes on to say: "Like the legal system of any large community, that of the early Church consisted for the greater part in regulations and obligations which were handed on orally, particularly during the three centuries of persecution, which made it difficult to fix them in writing."[19]

A motion was tabled at the Council of Nicaea (325 C.E.) to impose celibacy on bishops. The monk Paphnutius, who was himself celibate, spoke strongly against the motion because it would be the occasion for sexual temptation and irregularities. It seems the council refused to make celibacy obligatory for church officials but set the rule "according to an ancient tradition of the culture" that there were to be no marriages after the reception of an important office in the church. This has remained fundamental in both the East and the West. A variety of synods and councils over the years made rulings in respect to abstinence on the part of married clerics. The longer the church continued in history, the more the tradition of celibacy became a canon, a norm, and a confirming motive.[20]

On February 10, 385, a letter from Pope Siricius was sent to the Spanish bishop Himerius of the Province of Tarragona, in reply to the bishop's written request several months earlier to Pope Damasus, who had died in 384. An excerpt from that letter reads as follows:

> We have indeed discovered that many priests and deacons of Christ brought children into the world, either through union with their wives or through shameful intercourse. And they used as an excuse the fact that in the Old Testament—as we can read—priests and ministers were permitted to beget children. Whatever the case may be, if one of these disciples of the passions and tutors of vices thinks that the Lord—in the law of Moses—gives an indistinct license to those in sacred Orders so that they may satisfy their passions, let him tell me now: why does [the Lord] warn those who had the custody of the most holy things in the following way: "You must make yourselves holy, for I am Yahweh your God" (Lev 20:7)? Likewise, why were the priests ordered, during the year of their tour of duty, to live in the temple, away from their homes? Quite obviously so that they would not be able to have carnal knowledge of any woman, even their wives, and, thus having a conscience radiating integrity, they could offer to God offerings worthy of his acceptance. Those men, once they had fulfilled their time of service, were permitted to have marital intercourse for the sole purpose of ensuring their descent, because no one except [the members] of the tribe of Levi could be admitted to the divine ministry.[21]

In the 380s it was still an open question whether the integrity that had come to be associated with consecrated virgin women would spill over into the ranks of the clergy. A current of opinion had long existed that favored perpetual continence for senior clergy as a visible symbol of the sacred nature of the Catholic priesthood. This idealistic theory was one thing but actual practice was quite another. St. Ambrose (bishop of Milan from 374 to his death in 397) came to realize that the best that could be expected of bishops and priests was for them to commit to postmarital celibacy at ordination, that all that could be demanded of the average man was that he should have already had children and not continue to have more. In his writings Ambrose adverted to a clear hierarchy: "Every day, in the readings of the Scriptures, and in the preaching of the bishops, the church proclaims praise for marital morality, but the glory goes to virginal integrity." Married sexuality lay in the shadow of the virgin state, the highest pinnacle of Christian virtue.[22]

On June 16, 390, several bishops met in Carthage, North Africa, to discuss a variety of disciplinary matters. The meeting was presided over by Genethlius, metropolitan of the Proconsular Province. Little is known about him except that Augustine mentioned him and he is thought to have been quite prominent in the African episcopate. There is a suggestion that the meeting was not well attended, but the preface to the record of the meeting mentions two of Genethlius's colleagues, Victor of Abzir and Victor of Pupput. This modest synod of 390 evidently remained valid and was officially inserted in the great legislative record of the African Church, the *Codex Canonum Ecclesiae Africanae*, which was compiled and promulgated in 419 during the time of St. Augustine. From this codex we have this excerpt:

> Epigonius, Bishop of the Royal Region of Bulla, says: The rule of continence and chastity had been discussed in a previous council. Let it [now] be taught with more emphasis what are the three ranks that, by virtue of their consecration, are under the same obligation of chastity, i.e., the bishop, the priest, and the deacon, and let them be instructed to keep their purity.
>
> Bishop Genethlius says: As was previously said, it is fitting that the holy bishops and priests of God as well as the Levites, i.e., those who are in the service of the divine sacraments, observe perfect continence, so that they may obtain in all simplicity what they are asking from God; what the apostles taught and what antiquity itself observed, let us also endeavor to keep.
>
> The bishops declared unanimously: It pleases us all that bishop, priest, and deacon, guardians of purity, abstain from [conjugal intercourse] with their wives, so that those who serve at the altar may keep a perfect chastity.[23]

By about the end of the fourth century, a new church liturgical law forbade sexual intercourse in the night before communicating at the Eucharist. Evidently married priests had long observed this practice. The origin of the law of abstinence for married priests lies in Rome at the end of the fourth century; the only question is whether it happened under Pope Damasus (366–384) or Pope Siricius (384–399). It was about this period that the Western churches began to celebrate the Eucharist daily, which meant that abstinence from sexual intercourse became a permanent condition for married priests. The dominant reason for the introduction of this law of abstinence was "ritual purity." However, married priests were forbidden to send away their wives as not only abstinence but also living together in love with their wives was an obligation by canon law.[24] This is an important issue of justice in light of the fact that marriage was not yet a universal formal sacrament of Catholic Christianity.

Upper-class bishops in various regions felt they owed male heirs to their family and to their city. Synesius of Cyrene wrote to the patriarch of Alexandria in 410, to make plain that he would consent to act as bishop of Ptolemais only on the condition that he would be allowed to continue to have intercourse with his wife, saying that he would not be separated from her nor would he associate with her surreptitiously like an adulterer, because he desired and prayed to have virtuous children. About the same time, the bishop of Ephesus was not so diplomatic when he simply took his wife out of the convent where she had retired.[25]

Prior to his conversion to Catholicism, Augustine was an adherent of Manichaeism, which was later declared a heresy by the church. This was a dualistic school of thought. It held that humans are basically evil, locked in a perpetual conflict with good, and it denied the concept that we are wonderfully made and basically good. Augustine was remarkable for his genius and for his influence upon Western European civilization. Although Augustine repudiated Manichaeism, the cultural climate of his time and its antiquated understanding of human sexuality continued to pervade his thinking. Unfortunately, the longer the thinking that espoused celibacy perdured, the more entrenched and confirmed this limited theology became. In fact this error led to another error, namely, that the celibate state came to be regarded as a more holy state than the married state. We shall see this in a later chapter.

In Augustine's first decade as a bishop in Africa, he was in a different moral and religious environment than that of the Milan of Ambrose and the Italian and Gallic areas of Jerome's influence. The African clergy had studiously avoided excessive asceticism, and Augustine moved in more of an all-male world. While he imposed strict sexual avoidance on himself and his own clergy, he was not an alarmist and he was not preoccupied with celibacy. On a deeper level his priorities and those of the Christian piety of Africa in general differed from those advocated by the Italian admirers of virginity. Martyrdom always represented the highest peak of human heroism for Augustine. It was for him a far greater sign of God's grace to have triumphed over the bitter fear of death than to have triumphed over the sexual urge. Many African martyrs were married women and mothers of children as were Perpetua and St. Crispina of Theveste. When Augustine was writing to African nuns cautioning them never to look down on married women, Jerome could say that even the blood of martyrdom was barely able to wipe away "the dirt of marriage" from a Christian woman. Neither Augustine nor his Christian contemporaries found a way to suggest that sexual pleasure might enrich the relations between a husband and wife. About the year 401, Augustine went out of his way to distance himself from the high ascetic views of Jerome on marriage and virginity. These views were upsetting to Carthaginian Christians, to whom it seemed that upholders of the ascetic sensibility could defend their views only by denigrating marriage. Augustine's sermons were sensitive toward married couples and notably free from any icy tone. However in his *City of God*, Augustine created a darkened humanism with a distrust of sexual pleasure. This was a heavy legacy bequeathed to later ages.[26]

The church's views toward human sexuality dominated medieval thought and remained largely unchanged since the time of Augustine. The Middle Ages are mute testimony to the "heavy legacy" of marital sexual repression during the "childhood" of Christianity. It points up the fact that despite his genius and his formidable contribution to Christianity, neither Augustine nor any other human being is ever "fully arrived" in the sense of having all the answers.

One of the last and most relentless critics of Augustine was Julian, bishop of Eclanum in southern Italy. He was almost a generation younger than Augustine. Julian married while a young man in minor orders, around 400–403. His wife may have died or may have retired to a convent when Julian became a deacon about the year 409. Eventually Julian followed his mentors into a life of postmarital continence and he had long been continent by the time he wrote against Augustine. Julian wrote to defend the sexual urge "not as some outstandingly good thing, but as a drive in our bodies made by God." In his theory sexual desire did not have to be renounced at all. It was in no way corrupted. He posited that the sexual urge in married intercourse was no different from that with which God had first endowed Adam and Eve. He acknowledged that sexual desire at times would need to be controlled but could never be described as "fallen."[27]

The pessimistic view of human sexuality that dominated the early church impacted the "purpose" of marriage that was essentially held since the time of St. Augustine. This was eight centuries before marriage was regarded as a sacrament. The primary purpose of marriage since Augustine's time all the way to 1965 was *"the procreation and education of children."* Not until the theological purpose of sexuality in marriage was questioned at the Second Vatican Council, did it receive a revised broader context. It now includes *"the good of the spouses."* This was promulgated in the Pastoral Constitution on the Church in the Modern World (*Gaudium et Spes*).[28]

The more that I have thought about this, the more I have wondered why such an antiquated theological understanding of marital sexuality prevailed for so long. The reality is that most of the world was neither questioning nor open to such questioning. A raised social consciousness arises as an evolving awareness, and much of the world was absorbed in more primitive understandings of marriage and sex. Certainly untold millions of married couples during the intervening centuries undoubtedly came to look upon their mutual good as ranking equal with making babies. But this was not until modern times, since for many centuries couples married out of obligation because of arranged marriages, with exchanges of property including women as chattel, and for the legitimizing of children. As a more authentic Christian concept of marriage evolved, it is possible that some of the married clerics understood the "good of the spouses" element of their relationship, but they were precluded from theologizing or expressing it.

This brief account of the earliest centuries of Christianity reveals the lengthy struggle in the church to attribute spiritual and moral values to human sexuality. When church leaders began to make written rules for clerical sexual behavior, they did so in the face of a prevailing conglomeration of views, based on primitive understandings of human sexuality and their associations with ascetically motivated spiritual practices. It is noteworthy that attempts by church leadership to limit or repress sexuality uniformly for every individual married cleric has never ceased to be challenged and, frankly, to be more or less ignored. This is an important consideration because it is a manifestation of the Spirit of God consistently operating within the people of God—a valid sign of the times. Most noteworthy of all is the inconclusiveness of the struggle and, as it turned out, the ineffectiveness of seven centuries of the imposition of the law of abstinence on married clerics in the Western church from the end of the fourth century to the early twelfth century.

My reference to the "childhood" of Christianity follows St. Paul's teaching that "in one Spirit we [are] all baptized into one body" (1 Cor 12) and his description of how a child talks, reasons, and thinks (1 Cor 13:11). The 1139 ruling making celibacy compulsory for all clerics signaled a new phase in the life of the church. By implication it confirmed the experience of the first millennium, significantly and drastically. It was the beginning of a new era of clerical responsibility in the life of the church.

3

MY ADOLESCENCE

Hear, my son, your father's instruction, and reject not your mother's teaching.

Proverbs 1:8

The first overt indication of my interest in becoming a Catholic priest was when I was living in Kamloops. I was thirteen years old, in grade eight at St. Anne's Academy. I was an altar boy, serving mass at Sacred Heart Church—later Sacred Heart Cathedral. I wrote to Christ the King Seminary in New Westminster, British Columbia. I received a reply from the Reverend Luke Eberle who became the abbot of that Benedictine seminary. I remember him writing to the effect that not only would he like to see me attend the seminary but also he thought there was a possibility we were related! Despite his positive answer it didn't seem right at my age to be leaving home. I discussed it briefly with my mother. Her response was not overly encouraging. I talked with my friend in class who had also written. We both decided not to enter.

Our teacher at the time was Sister Monica Marie. We were quite a handful for her, but she was wonderful with a class of thirty students and we really did learn. Because of our age the sisters did their best to keep tabs on things. Sister Mary Ethelind was the principal. One of her rules was "no throwing snowballs." One day, after another student and I had thrown a few snowballs during lunch hour, the principal came into class right at 1:00 P.M. and asked me what she had said would happen if a student threw snowballs. I replied, "that we would get the strap!" She said, "That's right. Now step up here. You're going to get it now!" Both the other boy and I received about five strokes on each hand in front of the whole class. We were quite embarrassed but otherwise unharmed.

I took piano lessons from one of the sisters after school for a couple of years. Later Bernie and I took part in the Kamloops High School Band practice on Wednesday afternoons. Mom had gone to see the bandmaster who agreed that we could attend the band practices at the high school even though we weren't attending there. When I had completed grade eight and Bernie grade nine, we left St. Anne's Academy and went to the public high school where we had a daily band class as a subject in addition to the Wednesday practices. Things were considerably different in high school. We seldom spoke to the teachers or paid them the same kind of respect that we were used to with the sisters. Dad got after us a number of times for the way we were acting and threatened to send us back to the convent if we didn't start behaving better. I think it was a little easier for my parents when they no longer had to pay the tuition at St. Anne's, and Mom had reluctantly gone along with our move to the high school, allowing that we would have more musical training.

In high school Bernie and I continued to serve mass at Sacred Heart. Usually we served the high mass on Sundays and we handled the incense and Latin responses as required. When the church became a cathedral, Edward Quentin Jennings was appointed the first bishop of Kamloops. For one year I worked for the bishop when I took on the part-time job of church janitor, which included stoking the coal furnace. To my embarrassment, one cold Sunday I failed to add coal to the furnace soon enough. The fire burned back into the coal hopper and caused coal smoke to filter up into the church. The bishop was upset and let me know that if I couldn't do the job he would get someone who would. Later I was a janitor for an office building adjacent to Passmore's Book and Gift Store. For a couple of years during high school I worked as a supply clerk and served part time as a retail store clerk selling books and gifts at Passmore's.

Because of our attendance at the only Catholic school in this city of ten thousand people and our involvement with other youth of our age as altar boys, the influence of the church was quite significant in our lives. The west was less Catholic compared to St. Boniface, and because the Catholic community was not all that large, we were well known and felt accepted there. Mom was a devoted Catholic and always stood up for the church. At the time we moved to Kamloops, things were beginning to change after the Second World War. People were coming back to Kamloops, which was a railway center for both the Canadian Pacific and the Canadian National railways. Business was beginning to expand and Mom and Dad seized the opportunity to rent rooms in the large two-story home they were buying. A former neighbor from St. Boniface and an acquaintance of Mom and Dad's who had returned from military service came to live in Kamloops and rented from Mom for a while. I had known his younger siblings but not this man. I heard him in conversation with Mom being critical of the bishop, who he said was spending a lot of time watching the blond waitress at a local café during his daily visit for a cup of coffee. Mom became very defensive and told this acquaintance that he could no longer stay at her house if that's the way he was going to talk, especially in front of her boys! Mom stuck to her position, and the man moved out soon after.

We were kept quite busy during those years, and still found time to learn to play pool, to go swimming in the Thompson River during summer, and to play with the City of Kamloops Elks Band as well as the Canadian Legion Junior Symphony Orchestra. The high school band and the orchestra traveled to music festivals in British Columbia. The Annual Okanogan Music Festival alternated among the cities of Vernon, Kelowna, and Penticton. I participated with the band in each of them. The orchestra also played in the B.C. Music Festival in Vancouver. My longest band trip was to a national festival in Guelph, Ontario. The Elks Band also took trips, usually to attend conventions of the Elks Lodge. I attended conventions with the band in Victoria and later in Edmonton. School was generally a good experience for me and some of the teachers were absolutely excellent. I could have been a better student, but I didn't do much homework and managed to get on well with minimum effort. Much of my accomplishment was playing the trombone. I became the lead trombone player in a section of ten trombone players.

Obviously this musical training was a big part of Bernie's and my life. I could never reflect upon this period of my life without alluding to one of my greatest mentors—Archie Nelson McMurdo, the bandmaster whom Mom went to see and who ultimately had a tremendous influence upon me and hundreds of young people in Kamloops. He established the Canadian Legion Junior Symphony Orchestra which was a 150-piece orchestra, and which required participants to attend Friday evening practices throughout high school. The high school band consisted of 100 students playing woodwind, brass, percussion, and string bass only. The orchestra added to that number the complete stringed instruments, i.e., violins, violas, and cellos. The Elks men's band held a weekly Wednesday evening practice, and consisted mainly of men supplemented by some eight or ten adolescent students willing and able to participate. This band was a forty-piece group.

When I was sixteen, Staff Sergeant Blackman of the RCMP Band came to the Wednesday afternoon band practice and auditioned me playing a solo with band accompaniment. He interviewed me and offered to accept me at age seventeen when the normal recruit age at the time was eighteen. Because I had skipped a grade I graduated from high school just before turning seventeen. At that time, Dad wanted to move to California, where he hoped his boys would be able to take up music professionally. Dad's sister lived in Los Angeles and our whole family visited her when I was in tenth grade. Dad finally received an offer for the sale of our house, which he accepted. My own feeling about the RCMP was that I wanted to join the RCMP to do police work rather than become a bandsman. I declined the staff sergeant's offer at that time. Bernie however met with Blackman and later joined the RCMP Band and served some 37 years in that band until his retirement.

During my last year in Kamloops, my high school girlfriend was Arlene, whom I was only allowed to date intermittently. It was an impressionable time for us. We talked about marrying one day, although Arlene was designated to attend nursing school for three years, and my intention was to return to Canada to join the RCMP. I remember staying out all night after the graduation dance, and being in a restaurant a couple of blocks from our house at 7:00 A.M., when my mother came in and dragged me out by my ear! Arlene and my chum Leroy and I had been driving around in a Model "A" Ford after the dance until we decided to have some breakfast. This was quite embarrassing for me but Mom didn't care about that. Most of our adolescent years she had to look after things at home and she did a good job.

Three of my brothers and I were born in Winnipeg, before we moved to Kamloops. My last brother, Bob, was born in Kamloops. He was eight years younger than Bill. My brother Chuck was between Bill and me. Dad worked the 3 P.M. to 11 P.M. shift as a crew dispatcher for the railway and Mom kept us quiet so Dad could sleep when we got up for school, and most of the time Dad was gone by the time we came home from school in the afternoon. Dad had been transferred from the "running trades" on the railway to the crew dispatcher job, after his medical exam revealed albumen in his urinalysis. Mom was quite protective of

Dad because of his health. We never had salt in our food, which was just as well, and Mom tried to make sure that Dad rested and most of the time she handled the discipline. On Dad's days off, however, he would lay down the law especially if he had received some reports from Mom that needed his authority!

When Mom became pregnant with Bob, I learned of this from one of the girls at school, who learned of it from her mother who had been in conversation with my Mom. I remember going home from school that day and getting after Mom for not telling us, and I recall that she was a little embarrassed. The next discussion I remember having with her was that if anything was to go wrong and it became a question of her life or the life of the child, according to the church the life of the child would take precedence. Wow! How impetuous and silly of me! I remember Mom telling me that she checked with Uncle George, her Jesuit brother, and he told her not to worry and just follow the instructions of the doctor! I attribute this to what I had received in religion class from the sisters at school. In one sense it reveals the kinds of things Mom had to deal with from her sons.

Raising five boys and being the sole organizer of the household as well as chief cook and bottlewasher was quite a task for my mother. By today's standards it would seem pretty formidable, but Mom handled it quite well. In addition to taking care of the six of us, Mom took in lodgers. She rented two suites upstairs, a single room on the main floor, and a couple of rooms in the basement. Her efforts to keep her boys under control were sometimes humorous when I look back on them. My older brother, Bernie, managed to try Mom's patience from time to time. He was usually in the lead in lots of our antics, and we let him bear the brunt of Mom's fury. One time, when we should have been paying attention to Mom, she threatened to take the broom to us. We taunted her by saying it wouldn't hurt anyway, until sure enough she smacked Bernie with the broomstick. The broom handle broke—only to provoke a great deal of laughter from all of us, including Mom.

As I was completing my last year in high school, the sale of our large two-story house was imminent. Mom and Dad were busy planning things and they shared with us the idea that we would travel on a railway pass to Winnipeg, then to Montreal to see relatives, then to Detroit where we would buy a new car and travel to Florida, and finally across the southern states to California where we planned to live. When the time to move came, I was very emotional about leaving my girlfriend and the town that held a lot of memories for me. I was quite sure I wouldn't remain in the United States but it was incumbent upon all of the family to move at that time and so we did. We stopped first in Winnipeg and visited with many of our relatives there. We continued to Montreal and visited with my Jesuit uncle George and my cousin Sister Louise, then a postulant with the Holy Name Sisters. We next traveled to Detroit where we bought a new Plymouth and drove to Florida where we visited with friends of my Mom and Dad. The trip was really wonderful, if not difficult at times because my younger brother Bob was still in diapers and traveling such a long distance by car in the heat of summer with two adults and five children was not always pleasant. In addition, Dad had picked up pneumonia during the course of leaving his work and selling all he had to pick up and move to a new country. In any event we made the trip safely, with Bernie and me helping Dad with the driving.

Dad negotiated the purchase of a new home in Torrance, California, while we all stayed with his sister in Los Angeles. Next, Dad negotiated the acquisition of a brand-new leased service station from Flying A Oil Company, and for the next year Dad, Bernie, and I began to build this business. It was slow going and we were subject to a lot of scrutiny from the oil company, and after a year and a half or so, during which time my Dad's health began failing, we left the business. I am sure Dad lost money in the process. In the course of that year both Bernie and I attended El Camino Junior College on a part-time basis. I played trombone with the football band and went on a number of trips with the team, and continued to foster the idea of returning to Kamloops to join the RCMP. I remember thinking that it would have been better for the three of us to take jobs rather than have us all work in the business without salary, even though it did sustain the family. I felt sorry for Dad, too, as the business did not take off well right from the start. The fact is that the operator who took over from us was able to realize a good return. In retrospect, the man who bought the house from my parents in Kamloops was able to double his money by selling that property to Canada Safeway, which demolished the house and built a new grocery store on the site. I am sure this was disappointing for Mom and Dad and it was for me too, because I would much rather have remained in Kamloops, and even if I left to pursue a career I would have been able to come back to visit my family and familiar surroundings. I understood later that it had been Dad's goal to move to the land of opportunity, and it took so long for him to be able to sell the house that someone else saw and took advantage of the value of the property.

The summer before I turned eighteen I suggested to Dad that he let me go and I would work my way back to Canada by getting a job serving gas in Las Vegas and Portland and eventually get to Kamloops. I remember him saying, "Like hell! If you and Bernie want to go, I will drive you back and when I know you're safe the rest of us will come back here." I didn't fully appreciate Dad's position at the time, mostly because of my desire for independence. Dad did exactly that; he drove us back to Kamloops and we all stayed in Mom's uncle's hotel just as we had done in 1945 when we first moved to Kamloops. Dad encouraged Bernie and me to get jobs so that he would be able to head back. I was renewing acquaintances and probably taking my time so that finally Dad got after me, and I took a menial job shoveling coal from the railway boxcars into a truck and assisting in the delivery of this coal to the schools in preparation for the coming winter. An eye-opener for me was working alongside an older alcoholic laborer who smelled of booze but was able to out-shovel me.

About the second day on this job I went to the hotel to say goodbye to my parents and brothers. I met Mom who was dressed and leaving to attend morning mass. She had a tear in her eye, quickly gave me a kiss, and said goodbye. I went upstairs to Dad's room where my youngest brother was in bed with him. I said, "Well, I guess this is it, Dad!" Dad then propped himself up on his elbow and put his hand in mine and cried really hard. I didn't know what to do except to say goodbye and then I left to join my alcoholic coal-shoveling buddy. Ironically, we had to fill the coal bin of the Lloyd George School, where I first attended grade six in the fall of 1945. It was then the fall of 1953.

Bernie and I took up residence in the fire hall, where we became volunteer firemen. We were given free lodging with clean linen and towels each week, in return for attending fire and ambulance calls for which we were paid $2.00 per call. Our role was to assist the dozen or so permanent firemen on staff. It was exciting and gave us a home base with some of our friends. Meanwhile I applied to join the RCMP, and it took about four months before I was notified of my acceptance. My first real period of loneliness was upstairs in the fire hall, after my parents and brothers returned to California. There was a large games room with a couple of pool tables. I wasn't shoveling coal anymore and so was alone in this large room, listening to saxophone music. I have never felt such loneliness before or since. I think it was because I realized how much my family meant to me. More particularly, my Dad's response to my leaving was something I hadn't been prepared for despite my desire for independence. And there I sat, on my own, the door to everything near and dear to me now closed. It was a deep feeling of desolation. I am not sure I ever fully recovered from that. For years I could not even speak of my experience of saying goodbye to Dad without crying. Even now, forty-eight years later as I write these words, I am crying. I am sure I was angry with Dad for not having expressed his love to me earlier. Oh yes, I knew he loved me, but it just wasn't macho for males to express it. I made up my mind that I would tell my children that I loved them. Today, I look at the exhortation from Proverbs that introduced this chapter, and I conclude, "Yes, I heard my father's instruction. He did it well."

4

CELIBACY BECOMES MANDATORY FOR ORDINATION

> We also decree that those in the orders of subdeacon and above who have taken wives or concubines are to be deprived of their position and ecclesiastical benefice. For since they ought to be in fact and in name temples of God, vessels of the Lord and sanctuaries of the Holy Spirit, it is unbecoming that they give up to marriage and impurity.
>
> Second Lateran Council, no. 6

The law of celibacy in the Latin church was first stated implicitly in canons 7 and 21 of the First Lateran Council in 1123 and was then promulgated explicitly, sixteen years later, in canons 6 and 7 of the Second Lateran Council in 1139. This history reveals that the fundamental matter was a law of abstinence that existed from the end of the fourth century until the twelfth century. The law of celibacy grew out of the law of abstinence and was promulgated with the intention of making the seven-hundred-year-old law of abstinence effective.[1] The two relevant prohibitions from the First Lateran Council of 1123 are:

> 7. We absolutely forbid priests, deacons or subdeacons to live with concubines and wives and to cohabit with other women, except those whom the council of Nicaea permitted to dwell with them solely on account of necessity, namely a mother, sister, paternal or maternal aunt, or other such persons, about whom no suspicion could justly arise.[2]
>
> 21. We absolutely forbid priests, deacons, subdeacons and monks to have concubines or to contract marriages. We adjudge, as the sacred canons have laid down, that marriage contracts between such persons should be made void and the persons ought to undergo penance.[3]

These prohibitions reveal that the ritual law of abstinence gradually became more stringent. The explicit canons that rendered celibacy "mandatory" from the Second Lateran Council includes canon 6 cited above and the following:

> 7. Adhering to the path trod by our predecessors, the Roman pontiffs Gregory VII, Urban and Paschal, we prescribe that nobody is to hear the masses of those whom he knows to have wives or concubines. Indeed, that the law of continence and the purity pleasing to God might be propagated among ecclesiastical persons and those in holy orders, we decree that where bishops, priests, deacons, subdeacons, canons regular, monks and professed lay brothers have presumed to take wives and so transgress this holy precept, they are to be separated from their partners. For we do not deem there to be a marriage which, it is agreed, has been contracted against ecclesiastical law. Furthermore, when they have separated from each other, let them do a penance commensurate with such outrageous behavior.[4]

The view that the law of abstinence was being observed only very superficially by married priests can be seen in the writings of the councils held between the fifth and the tenth centuries. Church leaders were aware of this, and after a variety of vain attempts to make it more strict by sanctions and economic penalties they resorted to the most drastic means of all—a prohibition against marriage. Only from that time (1139) did marriage become a bar to the priesthood, so that only the unmarried could become priests. When the ritual law of abstinence was turned into a law of celibacy, the thinking behind that action was based on an antiquated anthropology and an ancient view of sexuality.[5]

It is not surprising that there is still an underlying outlook in some levels of the Roman Catholic Church, particularly those that are exclusively celibate, that sexuality and sacramental ministry are incompatible; however, the perception of some inherent impurity in the expression of human sexuality is diminishing. This spiritual archaism is slowly but surely moving toward complete elimination.[6] For more than eight hundred years in the Western Catholic Christian tradition, marriage has been closed to all those in holy orders. This means that a man wishing to become a priest today cannot be married. He must be a bachelor, or a widower, or more recently a formerly married man who has been civilly divorced and has received a declaration of invalidity from a church tribunal. In the latter case, however, some bishops have refused to ordain formerly married men who have been granted a declaration of nullity. Marriage was actually precluded for all men who were ordained to the orders of subdeacon and above by the decree of the Second Lateran Council.

Historically speaking, it is clear that even the 1139 law of celibacy is governed by the antiquated and ancient conviction that there is something unclean and slightly sinful about sexual intercourse (even in the context of sacramental marriage). A secondary reason for the law of celibacy was the fear that church property would be passed on through inheritance to the sons of priests. Nevertheless, the ritual law of abstinence was the only decisive and the only determinative element in ecclesiastical legislation.[7]

There were voices urging the church to moderate its traditional discipline of obligatory celibacy in the period before the Protestant Reformation. William Durandus the Younger discussed the problem of clerical incontinence in preparation for the Council of Vienne held in 1311. Citing the fact that various councils and Roman pontiffs had legislated against concubinage to no avail in improving clerical morals, he asked whether it would be expedient for the West to follow the practice of the East with regard to the vow of continence. The canonist Panormitanus (1386–1445) strongly endorsed priestly marriage. He reasoned that continence was not part of the substance of orders for secular clerics nor of divine law, otherwise married Greek clerics would be sinning! He concluded that not only did the church have the power to make continence optional but that it would be for the good of souls to do so. Another person, Aeneas Silvius, the future Pius II, evidently favored a change in this ecclesiastical discipline before he became pope. In one of the official documents relating to the agenda of the Council of Constance (1414–1418), Cardinal Zabarella stated that if they could not deal effectively with concubinage, it would be better to permit clerics to marry.[8]

Eventually Luther, Zwingli, Calvin, and other reformers forced the Council of Trent to consider the question at length. About that time, the emperor Ferdinand, the duke of Cleves, and Duke Albert of Bavaria pressed the Holy See to allow priests to marry. Their urging was an effort to conciliate the Protestants. Although Rome did not yield the point before the Council of Trent would debate the matter, on August 31, 1548, at the instance of Emperor Charles V, the papal nuncios in Germany were empowered to recognize the marriages of priests who sought to marry provided those dispensed would cease to function as a priest. This faculty to dispense was extended to England's Cardinal Pole in 1554 when Catholicism was restored under Mary Tudor. In February 1563 the long postponed subject of enforced clerical celibacy was discussed at the twenty-third session of the Council of Trent. Canon 9 of that council was proposed as follows: "If anyone says that matrimony must be placed before virginity or celibacy, and that it is not better and more blessed to remain in virginity or celibacy, than to be joined in matrimony, let him be anathema." Changes were made to speak of the "conjugal state" and the "virginal state," and ultimately this was approved in November 1563.[9] Clearly Trent was to counter the reform, and its effect upon the church was to establish rigid laws designed for conformity. Canon 9, when viewed in the post-Vatican II era, illustrates that rigidity: celibacy came to be regarded as a more holy state than the married state.

The Council of Trent was successful, as no previous council had been, in bringing about a general observance of the discipline of celibacy. Perhaps the single cause of its effectiveness can be attributed to the seminary system, which it inaugurated. It was with rigorous training beginning at a young age, carried on over a long period of time under constant supervision and careful selection, that this was accomplished. Many priests alive today began their preparation in a junior seminary at age fourteen. The success of Trent was therefore not immediately apparent. In fact, clerical celibacy was far from settled in many Catholic areas. The Tridentine decrees long remained unpromulgated and ineffective in many countries because of political interference. In many places clerics persisted in their accustomed styles of living. The Synod of Osnabruck in 1625 blamed the stubbornness of the heretics on the immorality of the clergy who openly supported their children from church patrimony. In 1631 a Synod at Cambray suggested that the secular arm be called upon to remove concubines of the clergy. In 1652 the bishop of Munster complained that his clergy persisted in concubinage to the scandal of the faithful. During the seventeenth century hundreds of books dealing with celibacy poured from the presses of Europe. Clearly Trent had not buried the issue. Individuals persisted in challenging the church's stand regarding celibacy, and the French Revolution at the height of the Enlightenment moved the question from the theoretical to the practical arena. One of the first efforts at reorganizing the church after the revolution was directed to restoring celibacy. The concordat with Napoleon in 1801 left internal discipline of the church to itself. After its signing, however, 3224 priests and religious petitioned either for reinstatement or for regularization of their marriages. More than two thousand of these chose marriage.[10]

Agitation continued in opposition to imposed celibacy, so much so that Pope Gregory XVI took note of it in his encyclical *Mirari Vos* of August 15, 1832, in which he called for support against a "most detestable conspiracy against clerical celibacy." In November 1846 Pope Pius IX also wrote in his encyclical *Qui Pluribus* about the "vicious conspiracy," and a few years later he denounced those who asserted that marriage was a higher calling than virginity. Organizations were formed with a view to abolishing clerical celibacy. One such organization was closely tied to the national unification movement, which disrupted the First Vatican Council and ended the temporal power of the papacy. This was the first ecumenical council since Trent and it actually debated the question of celibacy to some extent but never made any decision; nor was the issue brought to a vote. After the council ended abruptly, a number of Catholic priests and laity, chiefly in German-speaking areas, refused to accept the decrees on papal infallibility and primacy. In September 1871 at Munich three hundred representatives met to organize the Old Catholic movement. Similar congresses continued and a number of autonomous episcopates were established that have as a common doctrinal basis the Declaration of Utrecht. The Old Catholics in Switzerland abolished compulsory celibacy in 1875, modified it with conditions in Germany in 1877, and abolished it in Austria in 1880 and in Holland in 1922.[11]

Many other theologians found themselves at odds with the church over this thorny issue. In 1907 Pope Pius X noted in *Pascendi* that one of the goals of the Modernist movement was to eliminate sacerdotal celibacy. Treatises of two French priests, Dolonne and Claraz, were soon placed on the index of forbidden books. Baron Friedrich von Hügel was a great lay theologian and loyal friend of the leading Modernist priests Alfred Loisy and George Tyrrell. Von Hügel looked upon both marriage and celibacy with high esteem and was willing to grant that "certain modifications of the discipline [of celibacy] now required by the Roman Catholic Church in its Latin rite may be seriously desirable." Von Hügel, however, refused to allow any priest who had married become part of the movement with which he was associated. He held that the celibacy question demanded very delicate handling and that those who had resolved it for themselves had "disqualified themselves for any really useful leadership in the particular work we have at hand." After World War I the

Jednota movement of priests in Czechoslovakia asserted their right to marry and sent a delegation to Rome to gain the abolition of celibacy. In 1920 Pope Benedict XV strongly refused and added the view that they should not entertain any hope that the church would ever abolish it. The priests then proclaimed their independence from the Holy See and established a national church. The present controversy surrounding mandatory celibacy goes back to Pope John XXIII's 1959 announcement of Vatican II. An Italian Dominican R. Spiazzi commented about the forthcoming council and published some objections to celibacy. He quickly pledged his own support for the tradition, but his publication unleashed a torrent of articles, books, and surveys that followed.[12]

This chapter illustrates unequivocally the resistance over the centuries to mandatory celibacy for secular priests. Superceding any other "sign of the times" is the clear and unrelenting opposition to the church's discipline of enforced celibacy.

5

MY FIRST CAREER

When I became an adult, I put an end to childish ways.
1 Corinthians 13:11b

Leaving home was the start of a different period in my life. I felt a strong sense of independence and the desire to go back to Canada to join the RCMP. The fact is that all the time I lived in California the desire to become a "Mountie" was uppermost in my mind. I used to dream that I was wearing the police cap with the yellow band, not the "Smokey bear" Stetson hat which was part of the dress uniform, but the day-to-day forage cap which I had seen the policemen wear in Kamloops since 1950, when the former British Columbia Provincial Police Force was taken over by the RCMP.

When I attended El Camino Junior College in Torrance, California, I took a class entitled "California Penal Code." A LAPD sergeant who was recovering from polio taught it. In order to take the class I needed a letter from the police chief of Torrance. Many of the students were preparing for careers in law enforcement, some with the FBI and others with the County Sheriff Department or the Highway Patrol. At seventeen years of age this course was a real eye-opener for me. Hearing about vice squad enforcement and various kinds of sexual deviancies and prostitution in Los Angeles was quite disconcerting. Perhaps the most critical thing that I learned was that as late as 1952 a peace officer in California could shoot to kill any escaping felon except a forger and that it would be considered justifiable homicide. In fact the instruction given in class was that whenever we needed to use a firearm in the course of duty as peace officers, we should not shoot to wound but aim for the biggest part of the suspect that could be hit! Ostensibly this was to minimize the danger to the public that would result from attempting the more difficult shot of trying to wound a fleeing suspect in populated areas.

Before moving with my family to California, I had read a book entitled *Men of the Mounted*. I came to know some of the RCMP members who were stationed in Kamloops. I returned to Canada in the summer of 1953 and soon left the initial job of shoveling coal and went to work for an auto dealership. When I worked at the auto dealership and served gasoline, some of the police cars would gas up there. Seeing the men in their uniforms driving in from patrol duty seemed more exciting than fixing tires and having dirty greasy hands all the time. It was while working there and living in the fire hall as a volunteer fireman that I submitted my application to join the RCMP. As it happened, my application process took about four months.

The owners of the auto dealership learned of my application and offered me a better position in the company with a view to keeping me in their employ. I worked as a cost accountant preparing repair invoices and dealing with customers for a short time, during which I sought advice from others concerning my desire to enter the police force. Most of the advice I received was positive, and so when I received a letter offering me engagement for a five-year period, I accepted. I was sworn in at the Kamloops RCMP Detachment on January 2, 1954, and immediately took the train to Vancouver for recruit training. I was assigned to F-18 Squad, made up of thirty new recruits from all over Canada between the ages of eighteen and thirty five. Another recruit squad was nearing completion of their First Part Training before being transferred to Regina for Second Part Training. In addition, a number of squads of former B.C. provincial policemen were receiving indoctrination training after having been absorbed into the RCMP. This training was given at the Fairmont Barracks of the RCMP in Vancouver.

Our First Part Training was completed in April 1954 and our entire squad was transferred to Ottawa for Second Part Training. This consisted of more advanced law enforcement subjects and equitation. Ottawa is a beautiful city, the capital of Canada. A cousin of my mother lived there with her husband, a Wing Commander in the Royal Canadian Air Force. The training was quite arduous especially the second part in Ottawa. A feature of the daily routine for all the squads in training—there were about eight squads in the Rockcliffe Training Depot in Ottawa—was to be "on parade" at 6:30 A.M. in fatigue uniform with our grooming kits under our arm. We were marched to the stables and had to take the horses out of their stalls to the water trough, while other men cleaned the stalls, took the manure out to the pile, placed hay and oats in the stall food bins, and swept the entire stable clean as a whistle. If the instructor found a tiny piece of straw, the entire stable was to be swept clean again! Obviously this was a kind of "boot camp" experience. We then marched back to the barrack building, were dismissed to shower and change our uniform to that required for the first class of the day, be it academic, physical training in the gymnasium, swimming in the pool, or equitation in the riding school in the center of the stables. Usually we had to change our uniform several times each day, and our barrack rooms were subject to inspection every day and to more detailed inspections at intervals with the men standing beside their beds.

Equitation was quite interesting for "city guys" not used to animals, and it was the part of the training that most appealed to me, because it was closely associated with the image of the "mounted police" about which I had read and to which I aspired. Entering the stable on frosty cool mornings, we were hit by a strong urine ammonia smell from some forty to fifty horses, and when it was our turn we had to enter the horse stalls and lead two horses to the water trough. We did this holding the side of the leather halter attached to the horse's heads, walking between the two horses in a long line of horses in front and behind, along the long concrete hallway leading to the water trough. Occasionally the horses would get a little out of hand and one might get kicked or stepped on by a horse's hoof, but eventually we got used to the task and were able to keep a semblance of control. The actual equitation training was in the large riding school with a tam bark (sand and earth) mixture, where we learned portions of the famed RCMP Musical Ride. We learned to make backward somersaults off the horse and to crawl underneath it. After each riding session we were required to groom the animal including care of its hooves, teeth, and eyes. From time to time one of the men was bitten or kicked by a horse. We had to develop a certain amount of courage and some ability to handle the horses.

At intervals the troop was required to do jumps on horseback, usually down a fenced alleyway where three jumps were erected, each about thirty inches high. The horses were all quite excited at this event and holding them in was always a chore especially for novice riders. The task was exacerbated by the fact that each rider had to tie the reins in a knot and cross the stirrups, and sit on the horse with arms folded while going over the jumps. At each man's turn, the horse headed down the alleyway at a full gallop. There would be no controlling or stopping the animal once it started down the alleyway. The horses seemed to relish this event and apparently could tell the novice riders from the experienced ones. Some men were able to remain mounted during the jumps. Usually at the height of the first jump my legs went straight out parallel to the ground while the horse continued through the balance of the jumps without me! On occasion our riding lesson was conducted outdoors in a large grassy area, which happened to be at one end of the Royal Canadian Air Force aircraft runway. Large military cargo planes taking off and landing nearby required the riders to maintain good control over the horses. We didn't always have the same horse to ride, and one day when I was assigned to ride a stallion and a plane went over, the horse took the bit in its mouth and took off at full gallop toward the runway. I remember the riding instructor hollering and berating me as I sat helplessly hanging on while leaving the rest of the squad behind, only to come sauntering back after the horse's "run" was over.

The less glamorous part of our training dealt with law enforcement in general and the history of the Force (as we referred to the RCMP) in particular. We were called to a variety of extra duties on a roster basis, to provide security for the entire training complex. Occasionally a number of us were seconded to bolster VIP security and this occurred for me during the visit of Prince Philip of Britain. He was a guest at Rideau Hall, the governor general's residence in Ottawa, and I served two or three shifts on security duty there. This was the first time that we were issued bullets for our sidearm outside of target practice.

Graduation and posting throughout Canada occurred for most of the men in our squad in October 1954. The graduation included a marching demonstration by the thirty men in their red serge dress uniform, performing cavalry drill in rows of four men, the same as is performed on horseback during equitation. My loneliness manifested itself to some extent at this time, as I was proud of my accomplishment and I wished that some of my immediate family could be present. California seemed so far away from me in eastern Canada. Mother's cousin and her husband attended the ceremony, which I really appreciated, and during their visit they reminded me that I had not visited with them during my stay in Ottawa. I knew I should have visited them but I hesitated doing so partly being preoccupied with the training and socializing with squad mates during infrequent time off. It was easier, too, to keep my mind off family and busy myself with new people in the midst of this new enterprise.

I was one of three of our squad members who went to the Province of Alberta. When we arrived in Edmonton we were told of three openings in the province, and we more or less decided among ourselves where we would go. I had mentioned on the train from Ottawa that I wouldn't mind going to the Calgary area, so when one of the openings was in the Calgary Sub/Division, the other two colleagues agreed I should go there. One of them went to the Red Deer Sub/Division and the other to the Peace River Sub/Division. In a couple of days I was en route to Calgary where I lived in the barrack rooms on the eighth floor of the main downtown post office building. My duties initially consisted of escorting prisoners to the provincial jail, escorting mental patients to the provincial mental hospital, and escorting prisoners who had been sentenced to more than two years imprisonment to the federal penitentiary at Prince Albert, Saskatchewan.

In about three weeks I was transferred to Drumheller, a coal-mining town of five thousand people. The sergeant in charge of Drumheller Detachment came to Calgary to pick me up with my luggage. During the drive to Drumheller he kept asking me about my background and the more he learned about me the more he shook his head! He learned that I was just nineteen years of age. I had no prior police experience and I didn't even have a driver's license for the Province of Alberta. He made sure that I understood that the drinking age was twenty-one and that I would have to be on my best behavior while I became oriented to my new duties. As it turned out I really liked this posting. There were twelve members stationed there, mostly younger single men living in barracks, and our duties consisted of enforcing the Criminal Code of Canada and the Provincial Statutes, primarily the Highway Traffic Act and the Liquor Control Act. This was a temporary posting for three months during the convalescence of a senior member from surgery. I returned to Calgary for a couple of more months, but at the request of the sergeant in charge I received a permanent posting to Drumheller where I served until the fall of 1956.

During my stay in Drumheller I was much like the other constables except that I probably paid more attention to keeping out of trouble. The RCMP has always been a semimilitary organization with a lot of esprit de corps, and in our off-duty time we partied and imbibed alcoholic beverages. It concerned me, when I was under the drinking age myself and was required to prosecute under-aged individuals for Liquor Act infractions, that I could take advantage of the enforcement environment and drink without being prosecuted. On one occasion I mentioned this in confession to the pastor of St. Anthony's Parish, Father Jimmy Smith. He was a tall, hardworking, holy man. His words to me were to the effect that in my situation, providing that no other risks were involved, I was not obligated to inform on myself. In many ways I had to grow up fast during my tenure in Drumheller. It was as if one Halloween I was going around soaping windows, and the next year I was chasing Halloween vandals!

In December of 1954 my brother Bernie and I were called home because Dad had become quite ill. I arranged to take my annual vacation and Bernie and I took turns visiting Dad in the hospital. Dad recovered during the time we were there—he even said, "Yesterday I was a dead man, but now my boys have come back to me!" I had been able to give him the first drink of ice water that he had taken in several days. I was sure his recovery was a psychological response to our visit. Dad was able to return home and we enjoyed the time together. He told me they trained me well and that I was a good nurse! Unfortunately my three weeks of leave passed quickly and I had to return to duty. Dad came to the airport to see me off, and I knew I would never see him alive again. It was just before Christmas. Bernie remained on with the family.

When my flight arrived in Vancouver, I had to change planes for Calgary. I saw an RCMP car and was able to sit with the constable driving around for awhile. I had known him during training in Ottawa even though he had been in a different squad. In my emotional state, my association with the Force and with a colleague in familiar surroundings made me feel at home. I was grateful for this interval before boarding the plane for Calgary. I arrived in Calgary and went to the RCMP barracks to stay overnight. A party was in progress and I learned that they were celebrating the birth of a baby born to one of the constable's wives. The constable had about two years of service and had evidently married secretly because the rule at that time was that constables could not marry for the first five years of service. When we joined we knew that in order to marry members needed to have five years of service, be granted permission from the Officer Commanding, submit their intended spouse to a security check, and have at least $1200 cash or convertible assets in the bank. It is easy to see how an esprit de corps would develop among men with a common goal, in common circumstances living away from their homes, sometimes having to perform critically needed tasks. For those who aspired to that life, it was wonderful and exciting.

There were other occasions when I was concerned with the moral aspects of my duties. One of the assignments I had was to submit reports on Widows' Pensions and Mothers' Allowances. In more rural areas, the RCMP was often called upon to perform social services where the appropriate social service agency did not have an office. I came to know people during the course of this activity. One morning I received a call from a mother whom I had recommended for continued social assistance, asking me to come to her home because of a problem with her son. When I arrived the distraught woman explained that her son and a buddy had stolen a vehicle the previous night and drove it about fifty miles before they rolled it over. The two were not hurt but I interviewed them and checked back at the office to learn that a report had just been received from the owner of the stolen vehicle. I arrested the two youths, then sixteen years of age, and followed the usual criminal justice procedures. The penalty for vehicular theft at that time was a minimum of one year in jail. The youths pled guilty and were sentenced to the one-year term. Later one of the boys escaped from the medium security institution and served the rest of his term in the federal penitentiary. Neither boy had much of an opportunity to develop a sound moral character because of the environments in which they lived. I felt badly for the mother who reported them, yet I had to operate within the system. It was as if I had launched the boys on their careers of crime, because putting people in jail to my mind was akin to sending them to school to be a criminal. Within the police circles I had been successful, but the outcome bothered me. A couple of years later, however, the criminal justice system began to moderate, and the mandatory one-year jail sentence for car theft was abolished. Suspending of sentences with probationary supervision came into being—a much more human approach to dealing with offenders.

On April 17, 1955, my Dad died in California. I flew home on compassionate leave to attend the funeral. He was buried in Long Beach. At that time my three younger brothers were still at home, the youngest of preschool age. Dad was forty-eight years of age when he died. My mother handled things quite well. She moved from San Pedro to the Van Nuys area, returned to her former occupation as a secretary for a life insurance company, and continued raising the children. Bernie meanwhile had returned to Kamloops and enlisted in the RCMP Band. He completed his training in Regina, Saskatchewan, after which he was posted to Ottawa where he spent all of his service.

I continued my service in Drumheller. During my stay there I used to go ice-skating and it was there that I met a young woman named Irene. Irene was completing her senior year in high school preparatory to taking radiology training at a Calgary hospital. We began to go out together, notwithstanding the anticipated separation. In November 1956 I was posted to Gleichen, Alberta, located sixty miles east of Calgary. This was the center of the Blackfoot Indian Reserve, the second largest reserve in Canada. Most of the enforcement there had to do with the Federal Indian Act, which superseded the Provincial Liquor Act and which precluded any and all consumption of alcohol by native people of Treaty Status. As a result the practice evolved that the Treaty Indian people drank other substances that contained alcohol such as shaving lotion and frequently even rubbing alcohol.

It was in Gleichen that I was to have a unique conversion experience through the friendship of a wonderful, eccentric, holy priest. Its population was only about four hundred but Gleichen was the center for a large farming area. St. Victor's Catholic Church was located within the town, and I began attending there and met the pastor, Father Eugene Violini. He had two dogs, a large St. Bernard and a small Pomeranian, several cats, chickens, and a parrot. He inquired of my family and in a sense took me under his wing and even wrote to my mother. I started serving mass again on mornings when I was available. Eugene rekindled my earlier attraction to the priesthood as he led me to a deeper level of faith. I told him about my girlfriend Irene who was then in training at the Calgary General Hospital. He encouraged me in that relationship and ultimately instructed Irene in the faith and received her into the church. Irene and I were considering marriage and on one occasion I commented to her: "I guess I can never be a priest now!" "Did you want to be?" was her question. "Yes," I replied, "but now I want to marry you, so that's what we should do."

Lest this sound too impetuous, it is necessary to recall the Force's policy regarding marriage. A great deal of discernment went into our decision to marry. I had joined the Force when I was eighteen, and I felt that I wouldn't want to be married until I was twenty-three anyway, so the marriage policy didn't concern me at the outset. As it happened, I was twenty-one when Irene and I knew we wished to marry. The question then arose, do I remain in the Force or do I leave? My priest friend encouraged me to accompany him to Calgary where we would visit the Sisters of the Precious Blood, a cloistered group of nuns, and ask them to pray for my discernment. This was an unusual situation, a priest and a Mountie, both in "uniform," visiting the cloister. About a dozen sisters were behind the wooden lath divider and anxiously awaited our visit—the eccentric charismatic priest who was always a joy for them to receive as a visitor, and the policeman who probably added to their fascination. The sisters asked all kinds of questions about my need for discernment, and I think they were intrigued by the story of our romance as it connected with my career and potential marriage. The sisters agreed to make a novena prayer, for nine consecutive days, specifically for my intention.

Some six weeks later, the priest and I paid a return visit to the sisters. When we arrived I asked, "Well, what's my answer?" They laughed and replied that I would know in my heart what to do. I told them that I still wanted to marry Irene, but I wasn't sure what do about the two-year waiting period. The superior asked what was happening in my life, and I told her that I had received a notice that I would be transferred on May 13. Her immediate reply was: "That's the day when Our Lady appeared to the children of Fatima." This didn't give me an answer but for a person with a devotion to Mary, the Mother of God, this could be taken as a favorable sign in response to prayer. For months, Eugene had been encouraging me to ask the mother of Jesus to intercede for me, which I had been doing, so it was easy for me to view the date of the proposed transfer in a positive light. We returned to Gleichen. A couple of weeks later, Eugene told me that he had had a dream in which the Mother of God revealed to him Irene and me and several children. In the dream, he saw me in my police uniform. Irene and the children and I were apparently living close to my work. I asked how many children, but he didn't know. The only suggestion Eugene could offer was that he felt God was saying I should marry Irene and I should stay in the Force. My discernment was difficult. I really loved the Force, but the long hours and the cold winters made leaving the Force seem feasible. However, Eugene's dream was more significant and I discussed this with Irene, and together we decided to accept these signs and to embark on a two-year engagement. Our engagement was liturgically celebrated in a nuptial betrothal, in which the engagement ring was blessed and our mutual promise to marry was expressed in church, in the presence of her family and our friends.

The discernment period had been informative because I learned more about the Force's policy of temporary celibacy during a conversation with a senior member. I had escorted a couple of prisoners from Gleichen to the Calgary Guardroom. After booking the prisoners, the corporal on duty said: "I hear you're getting married, Ron." I confirmed this and the corporal commented, "I would never wait again!" I asked him what he meant, and he told me that when he joined the Force the rule was that the men could not marry until they had completed twelve years of service. Later it was reduced to seven years, and still later to five years—which was the case when I joined. The corporal told me that he was thirty-two years old by the time he married, and he said "Look at me, I'm ready to go to pension and I'm still having to take my kid to hockey!"

At one time I knew seven RCMP members who were married "without permission" in the Calgary Sub/Division. Among the members this became common knowledge and nothing much was said until one day the situation was reported and the seven RCMP members appeared in an "Orderly Room" judicial proceeding pursuant to the federal RCMP Act. They were each fined $150 and dismissed from the Force as unsuitable. This was an incredible loss to the Force, which by this time had a considerable investment in these men. The men all went immediately to other police forces, some to a provincial police force and some to city police forces. It wasn't too much longer before policy changes were made and the rather dated and prejudicial requirement to remain single for a set period of time was abolished.

In my time in the Force, to be a member of the Masonic Lodge in some areas at least helped one to be part of the "in" crowd. It could even be a positive influence for promotion. The Force retained a British heritage. It was initially named the North West Mounted Police, later was honored by the change to Royal North West Mounted Police, and in 1932 the change to its present title Royal Canadian Mounted Police. The traditional religious and moral values flowed from the Anglican persuasion manifest in its chapel in Regina and in its code of policies, or regulations. The policy of temporary celibacy was originally adopted so that fifty percent of the Force could be single and thereby remain mobile and available for immediate postings to isolated regions.

To the contemporary mind a policy of temporary celibacy is an inconsiderate way to treat employees. When I was transferred permanently to Drumheller, the Sergeant told me at 4 P.M. that I was to be packed and on the bus by 7 P.M.! At the time I knew and accepted these conditions. The fact of the matter is that, at the Force's inception in the year 1874, it was to be a mounted cavalry-type organization with the mission to "maintain the right" over a huge wilderness area. Their semimilitary tradition took them into the modern era when mechanized transportation and communication became commonplace. Leaders were slow to renounce and revise policies consistent with the broad changes impacting the achievement of their mission.

In large organizations where recognition results from "compliance," new leaders tend to act on "the way it was" rather than "the way it is." Gradually, perpetuating the organization's tradition can become more important than perpetuating the organization's mission. Adherence to the traditions of the Force began to bind its members by constraining their behavior to customs that no longer worked in the changed environment. It wasn't until its anachronistic policy of temporary celibacy was rejected at the grass-roots level that it was changed.

I learned later that the Force wasn't the only agency that demanded temporary celibate living as a condition of employment. Some of the banking institutions in Canada required this of their employees who would take a posting to isolated areas. Also, in the United States it was common practice for women schoolteachers to remain unmarried during their teaching careers. In retrospect, such policies gave consideration to the plight of family members who would be subjected to isolated or demanding living conditions as well as the good of those being served by these professions. But in the face of changed social conditions, those policies ultimately infringed upon the common good of all, certainly on the right of people to marry.

Our two-year wait was marked by my transfers to the postings of Elk Island Park, Lamont, Edmonton, Mayerthorpe, and ultimately to Westlock, all in the Province of Alberta. There were many signs from the Blessed Mother that in my mind corroborated the earlier indications that we were following the will of God. For instance, at my first posting of Elk Island Park, my parish was Our Lady of Good Counsel in Skaro, Alberta, where I was able to render considerable help to the pastor, Father Zenko. Even the police car I was assigned was the characteristic baby blue color often associated with images of Mary. I never saw one of that color before or since! Irene meanwhile moved to Edmonton and took up residence in Rosary Hall, a home for single women run by nuns. This allowed Irene and me to see each other while I was in Edmonton, and then intermittently when I was transferred to Mayerthorpe and was able to travel to Edmonton. On a number of occasions we attended mass at Rosary Hall together.

While in Mayerthorpe I was the only available policeman to attend a fatal motor vehicle accident in which a priest had been killed. I met Archbishop Anthony Jordan who came to view the body after the accident. It was while I was in Mayerthorpe that Pope John XXIII announced the Second Vatican Council. It was there that I applied for permission to marry and satisfied all the conditions still required, and once the approval was granted I was informed that I would be transferred to Westlock, located some fifty miles north of Edmonton.

Because of the special friendship that I had enjoyed with Eugene Violini, I was able to question just about everything I could think of about the Catholic faith. Eugene had schooled me well in the year and a half I spent in Gleichen. He emphasized how significant example was in relation to the faith of the people. He said that when a priest "falls" he takes a lot of people with him. His pedagogy in many ways espoused the idea that a person in a public role such as myself in the police force had a responsibility to lead by example. Before leaving Gleichen, I was reported to RCMP headquarters for helping Eugene by taking tickets at his Sunday evening movies. The church was not licensed as a theater under the Provincial Amusements Act, a thought that hadn't really occurred to me since we were not usually involved in direct enforcement of business licenses.

The Section NCO interviewed me about the complaint made against me. I explained my role in my off-duty time, which ostensibly was beneficial for the native people that attended even for the nominal fee that was charged. The investigating staff sergeant quite understood but made it clear to me that although I was free to help out in community endeavors, as soon as the legality of such an undertaking would be questionable I had to reassess my participation. The Force accepted my explanation and nothing came of the complaint. Eugene consoled me by telling me the complainant was a disgruntled, cynical parishioner and he described the experience as an instance of persecution in the cause of righteousness pursuant to the Beatitudes (Mt 5). I tended to agree with him since the local theater owner was not the complainant and at that time the public theater was not open on Sundays.

And so it was that I came to an overt practice of my faith, marked as I was, being in uniform and in public office, in the smaller Canadian communities where I was stationed. When I arrived in Westlock, the clergy that I came to know were somewhat bemused by my faith practices, which particularly for policemen were a little out of the ordinary. I was a daily communicant whenever possible and a supporter of the clergy in a variety of ways. When I would pass in front of a church, I made the sign of the cross in recognition of the presence of the Blessed Sacrament.

I frequently talked and visited with clerics. On one occasion, a young seminarian came to see me on the recommendation of his advisers. The seminarian was evidently concerned about the rule of celibacy, and he asked me for my views about marriage and priesthood. I had known some of his family members where I was previously stationed. We had a nice conversation. I wasn't sure if or how I may have helped him, but the seminarian went on to ordination and I took some satisfaction from that. Looking back on my past practices, I realize that our theology and our social customs have changed and my practices along with them. I learned, too, that there is a very real danger of becoming self-righteous rather than righteous, by such overt emphases on faith practices. For the most part, however, I would characterize some of my former faith practices as motivated by a mixture of sincerity and naiveté, rather than self-righteousness.

I think my membership in the Force helped me to hold any blatant self-righteousness in check, right from the time of the complaint made about me in Gleichen. Occasionally a fellow member would challenge me by criticizing priests for being hypocrites. Once a senior staff sergeant asked me why I went to church every morning. On another occasion I mentioned to a colleague that I had prayed with a native prisoner en route to jail. He severely chastised me, telling me I was out of line for having done so. I defended my action on the basis that the native person had been raised a Catholic and our conversation about faith and lifestyle was beneficial for the prisoner and lent itself to prayer.

Sometimes even the priests would question me. Once after members of our detachment had marched in a civic parade, Father Morrissette told me he had waited to see if I would make the sign of the cross when we passed in front of the church. I told him that I thought that would be inappropriate as I was "on parade." On one occasion after the prosecution of a local businessman that I had initiated, Monsignor Rooney took issue with me suggesting that the liquor act violation carried too severe a penalty and my interpretation smacked of the letter rather than the spirit of the law. I defended myself at the time and the case proceeded, but it made me question and eventually I came to understand more clearly what Rooney had been trying to tell me.

6

THE PRIESTHOOD THAT I KNEW

> You are a priest forever, according to the order of Melchizedek.
>
> Hebrews 5:6

My knowledge of priesthood came from my earliest years and continued up through my young adult years until I went to the seminary in my fifties. I have already mentioned seeing my Uncle George come to visit us in our home in St. Boniface. Usually he came in his cassock. I remember him opening it to illustrate for the family, and I exclaimed, "Oh! You have pants and a shirt underneath!" Mom and my brother were there and they laughed. He would give us his blessing when he left. I next came to know the priests at St. Boniface Cathedral. They took us on long hikes during winter days that ended with a banquet and prizes. They taught us how to say the Latin responses to the prayers at mass. They guided me in serving mass and at those special celebrations when a bishop or cardinal attended. I served as a miter bearer, crosier bearer, and even trainbearer when Cardinal Villeneuve came from Montreal. This was the church triumphant with all its regal trappings. I wore white gloves to hold those special signs of hierarchical office. All of us at the St. Boniface Cathedral wore cassock, surplice and biretta. Sometimes the Franciscans in their brown habits, barefoot in sandals and with halo tonsure haircut, were in attendance, but I never got to know any of them.

When we moved to Kamloops, there were fewer altar boys and we got to know the priests quite well. Father Massey, Father Towne, Father Murtagh, and Father Quigley all served under Bishop Jennings. I used to take my weekly turn serving daily mass for each of those priests. Each of them made an impression upon me that was generally good. As long ago as the 1950s Father Massey offered advice about life. He commented to me that a man should be at least twenty-eight years old before marrying and have several thousand dollars in the bank. Father Towne reportedly was from Texas. He treated the altar servers well. On one occasion he took four or five of us on a hike to the summit of Mt. St. Paul, a well-known landmark in Kamloops. He provided us with sodas as we rested at the summit, while he himself had a beer. We kidded him about it and his response was that we had "pop" while he was having "bop"! Father Murtagh was from Ireland and was always helpful and a good friend. When he was transferred, I was disappointed. I never saw him again and I felt his loss for some time. Father Quigley had earlier served in Japan and was a bit of a maverick. Once when some of us altar servers were told to sit on the altar steps of the marble altar, he told us we should not do that because the marble was cold and we could get piles. He felt we were not being treated well!

Later when I joined the RCMP, Father Massey was the pastor of the closest Catholic church to the Fairmont Barracks in Vancouver. After mass one Sunday he expressed surprise that I had joined the Force. He counseled me to keep attending mass, because often when young men join the police force they quit going to church.

From these earlier experiences with priesthood, I moved on to the experiences with priests during my many transfers with the RCMP. In Drumheller Father Lemire was the associate pastor to Father Jimmy Smith. Both were great men. By this time I held priests in high esteem. They were good and generous men who gave up marriage and family to serve the wider family of God. I always respected them. I had sung with the choir briefly in Kamloops. I did this briefly in Drumheller as well. Those days saw four-part harmony choirs singing mostly in Latin. With my move to Gleichen, and my acquaintance with Father Violini, priesthood took on a new dimension. I helped him by typing the Gestetner template for his Sunday bulletins. I began to be with him most days for mass and sometimes for meals or for evening visits. One day during Sunday mass he asked me to take over the choir. I did so mostly because of my ten years of musical experience with bands and orchestras plus some choir experience. The choir members were very supportive, out of respect, I thought, because I was a policeman in their community—a fact that pleased them.

Eugene spoke highly of Father Jimmy Smith, who by that time had moved to Calgary and was then the chaplain to the cloistered Sisters of the Precious Blood. He told me that only a really holy priest is generally selected to chaplain a cloistered community. Father Armand Lemire had been Eugene's altar boy some years earlier and Eugene was quite proud of Armand. Eugene gave me most of my knowledge about the church, because of the unique friendship we shared. He told me many stories of events during his service as a priest—some were quite incredible. It was amazing to me to see this man in a small country parish, telling me these incredible things, yet being relegated as it were to less important assignments by the bishop. He had numerous health problems and struggled because of this during his seminary days. There was no mistaking however that he learned well what he was taught. By the time I knew him he had been ordained for more than twenty-five years. I was able to question many aspects of my faith during the times I visited with him, and he was able to give me great answers indeed. During our private conversations, Eugene was very critical of priests who either were careless in the practice of their ministry or did not continue on with the priesthood. I was always struck by his dedication and tireless efforts in the service of his parish. We frequently prayed the rosary together and he was faithful to his daily recitation of the divine office.

Eugene had some quaint spiritual practices. His church contained numerous statues of saints. When Irene first saw the rather small church with its many statues, she commented to me that it seemed cluttered. For every one of the statues, Eugene had a story and loved to tell them. He had a medal or two on the collars of his pets, usually of St. Rock, the patron saint of animals. He was especially outspoken on issues of justice. The movies he showed on Sunday evenings were partly as catechesis and partly to provide a wholesome activity. He rented all kinds of classic movies and charged a nominal fee to cover his costs. The parish itself was quite small and did not provide an abundance of income. When Irene took instructions from Eugene to become a Catholic, he arranged that she would spend an entire Saturday with him, doing household chores and cooking while he talked about the faith. After three such Saturday sessions, one of which included his "ring around the rosy" tour of the church, Eugene told me that her instructions were complete and now it would be up to me if in fact Irene would embrace the faith. Irene told me she no longer thought of the church as "cluttered" and subsequently she expressed a readiness to become a Catholic.

Irene's baptism took place on May 8, 1957. Gus, a Catholic colleague from the RCMP, with whom I was stationed in Drumheller, agreed to be her godfather. Eugene wanted Gus and me to attend in our red serge dress uniform. When I questioned this he asked, "When do you wear your dress uniform?" I replied, "Mostly when attending superior court trials as a witness or prisoner escort." Eugene said, "Well, the sanctuary is the royal courtyard of Our Lord!" He was very creative and a good liturgist. He presided at a public evening ceremony that included "conditional baptism" (no longer required of previously baptized Christians) and Irene's enrollment in the Sodality of Mary. It ended with Benediction of the Blessed Sacrament. I was in the choir loft leading the singing in my red serge, while Gus in his red serge stood beside Irene and her godmother, Mary, a friend from Drumheller.

With my transfer to Elk Island Park, I soon met Father Zenko, the pastor at Our Lady of Good Counsel parish in Skaro, a farming center some fifteen miles to the north. Zenko had been in the seminary with Eugene. He was a nice man, not much over five feet tall, but very dedicated. I attended some weekdays as well as Sundays during that summer, and Zenko asked me to help him, which I did. His housekeeper, Josie, invited me for breakfast on a few occasions. Zenko explained to me that he was having difficulty in his Polish national parish because the people were insisting on having all their liturgies in Polish, while at that time the church still conducted mass in Latin. He noticed that I usually attended church in uniform, since I was on duty in the National Park on Sundays, and he pointed out to me that in Poland the people not only respected the police, they feared them. He asked me to become part of the choir and to influence the group to sing in Latin with some Polish and English. I was able to do this with little difficulty, and the choir responded and taught me how to sing in Polish. I can still say the beginning of the Hail Mary in Polish.

At the end of the summer season, I was transferred to Lamont for a brief period while the corporal in charge was on vacation. While there I had the pleasure of meeting the Eastern Rite Ukrainian Catholic priest Father Dimytriuk. He introduced me to his wife and young daughter. We had a nice conversation during which he told me that he came to Canada as a displaced person after the war. His wife made a lasting impression on me; I think because she looked peaceful and happy. I remember her telling me that her father and his father were all priests going back for 450 years.

When the vacationing corporal and his family returned to Lamont, I was transferred to Edmonton and lived in the barracks there. I attended the Church of the Sacred Heart of Jesus, on 97th Street. It was across the street from the French Catholic Church of the Immaculate Conception. I came to know Monsignor O'Gorman, the pastor, as well as the two curates, Father McDonnell and Father Bonner. Within a few months I was transferred to Mayerthorpe, where I obtained room and board in a private home. Most of the time I worked farther west in the vicinity of the town of Whitecourt. Father Leonard was the pastor at Mayerthorpe and Father Tellier the pastor at Whitecourt.

Leonard had been a victim of tuberculosis and was not very strong. He lived in a poor parish and his rectory was under renovation most of the time that I was there. Most often on Sundays I was in Whitecourt, where I usually stayed in the hotel. I attended mass there and assisted Father Tellier with information that I had learned from Eugene, even to the point of providing some books that assisted Tellier with instructing new Catholics in the faith. I didn't get to know Father Leonard very well, except that Tellier and he were neighbors and went to confession to each other. Tellier spoke highly of Leonard, and it was Leonard who was killed in a traffic accident and Tellier who came to the scene to anoint him. His parishioners respected Leonard. He had been taking his suit coat to a farm woman to be sewn. He had eleven cents in his pocket and a scapular medal when he was killed. He was a dedicated servant of the church—another Christ, as we had learned was the role of the priest.

Before the Second Vatican Council, the spirituality of the diocesan priest was grounded in what was understood to be his ontological status as a priest of the church. This status conferred on him powers that were held in awe by believers and at least respected by nonbelievers. His priestly identity was concomitant with his power to consecrate, forgive, anoint, and bless. With these powers came the responsibility to lead a holy life appropriate to his priestly status. The source and fuel of the priest's spirituality was "saying Mass," praying the breviary, the rosary, and other devotions such as Benediction of the Blessed Sacrament. His ministry involved serving the poor, visiting the sick, educating children, instructing converts, and preaching to his people. While the priest's spirituality was ministerial, it focused largely on the devotional and ascetical aspects of his inner life. He prayed so that he might be a good priest and serve God and the people well.[1] This description capsulizes the priesthood that I came to know largely through relationship and association.

What had attracted me to Eugene Violini was his eccentric ways. His domain consisted of the small white-steepled country church named after St. Victor and his living quarters at the rear of the church behind the altar. Sometimes he would walk down the main street of the village with his parrot on his shoulder. He generally didn't wear his Roman collar on weekdays but everybody knew him. He usually wore a ski-cap and a heavy black sweater and black slacks. One day walking by the pool hall, he overheard some rough language and he stopped and asked, "Who took my Master's name?" This was his nature and his reputation. His eyesight was limited and concerned him when he had to drive to his two rural missions. He befriended me and I responded by helping him and frequently driving him to the missions so he could say mass on Sundays— even though I would miss being with Irene in Calgary.

Suppressing my desire to be with Irene when I could have obtained a "pass" to be away from the RCMP detachment area was a sacrifice, a form of prayer that I offered for the grace of a good marriage. It was in keeping with the spirituality of the time: fasting from midnight before receiving Holy Communion, fasting from meat on Fridays, fasting during the Lenten season, and following the example of saints like the Curé of Ars, a humble parish priest, and Thérèse of Lisieux with her spirituality of "The Little Way."

Looking back on priesthood in rural Canada in the period of time approaching the Second Vatican Council, particularly after leaving Gleichen and my association with Eugene, I now realize that the priesthood was a demanding, staid, kind of role. Social customs then were more respectful of "people of the cloth" and of civil authorities. Priests and nuns did most of the work in the church. Even my helping Zenko contributed to maintaining the "pay, pray, and obey" modus operandi of church leadership, if I may use that expression. The spirituality of the day was influenced by the lives of saints who were held up as models to emulate, models which were austere and sometimes weird by today's standards. Finally, Catholics in that period of time were quite isolated from Protestants, were largely ignorant of their beliefs and practices, and were sometimes hostile to, and generally felt superior to, them. Because the scandal of Christian disunity was a major obstacle to spreading the good news of Christ, church unity became one of the major purposes for calling the Second Vatican Council.[2]

7

MARRIAGE AND FAMILY

Therefore a man leaves his father and his mother and clings to his wife, and they become one flesh.

Genesis 2:24

In May of 1959, I was transferred to Westlock, which was to be my first posting as a married man. The pastor of St. Mary's Church there was Monsignor Eugene Rooney, who served fifty years in the same parish. He was a great man, well known and respected by all in the community. Three associate pastors whom I came to know were Father Robitaille and Father Guerin who had come from Quebec, and Father Lucien Morrisette, a native Albertan. Both Whitecourt and Westlock were in the St. Paul (Alberta) diocese and they bordered the other parishes mentioned which were in the Edmonton archdiocese. St. Paul's was essentially a French-speaking diocese as most though not all of the communities it served were French speaking.

It was in Westlock when liturgies began to change that I was asked to lead the congregational singing from the front of the church. While in Westlock I met and supported Father Kinderwater, O.M.I., in his efforts to coordinate the political process and public vote necessary to establish a new Catholic school in Westlock. I started a Legion of Mary group in Westlock for which Robitaille was the spiritual director. Two other priests I came to know in Westlock were Malcolm and Colin Campbell. Their parents and their brother lived there, and though the two priests were stationed elsewhere they frequently visited Westlock. Monsignor Rooney, Robitaille, Colin, and Lucien all shared their thoughts and questions and gave me insights about priesthood and the church, which was then formulating its historic correctives that were to take place during the Second Vatican Council.

Irene and I married on June 6, 1959, at St. Victor's Church in Gleichen. My brother Bernie was best man. A young lady from Gleichen whom Irene got to know was the maid of honor. A half-dozen members of the Force came to Gleichen and formed a guard of honor crossing lances at the entrance to the church for us to walk under as we came out. It was a typical "red serge" wedding. My mother was unable to attend as she was living in California raising my younger brothers. In her stead, her two sisters and brother-in-law came from Winnipeg. One of my aunts was Helen, my godmother. The other was Cecile and her husband Tom. Tom had been my confirmation sponsor years earlier. We had a meal served in the church basement but chose not to have a dance or an extended celebration. Irene and I drove to Drumheller and spent the night at the home of a friend of her parents. The next day, before setting out on our honeymoon trip to California, we drove back to Gleichen to attend mass in the church where we had received the sacrament of matrimony. It was an auspicious start after the long period of waiting.

The trip to California was in a car borrowed from a constable at Mayerthorpe. Irene met my mother for the first time and my brothers Bill and Bob. Chuck had come to Gleichen before I left for Elk Island Park, and by the time I had married he had also enlisted in the RCMP, having followed Bernie, so that there were now three Eberley brothers in the Force. Irene and I settled in a small rented home in Westlock. We had agreed that Irene would not work outside the home. Our first child, Eugene, was born in Westlock on May 6, 1960. Ironically, on that day another constable and I were in court in Barrhead, thirty miles west of Westlock, involved in a trial taking children away from their mother. The other constable's wife was in hospital for the birth of her second child while Irene was there for her first child. After court I stopped for a visit at St. Anne's Church in Barrhead to light a candle and say a prayer for Irene and our new baby, as well as for the other mothers and their babies, including the children who were taken from their mother.

From the outset I worked fairly long hours, as my work usually took me west to the town of Fort Assiniboine and beyond to the Swan Hills Oil Field where some sixty oil-drilling rigs were active during the oil boom there. Irene was a dutiful wife, seldom complaining about the hours, and content to be at home especially after our son was born. Father Robitaille baptized our first child. Robitaille was a great singer and liturgist, and after the baptism he carried our son and laid him on the altar in front of the tabernacle after the manner of Christ's presentation in the temple. Naturally this was very meaningful for us. Eugene Rooney was pleased that we had named our son Eugene, initially after Eugene Violini and coincidentally after Eugene Rooney. Rooney gave us a tiepin with the name Eugene engraved on it, which he had received as a youngster.

Travel to Swan Hills was always an ordeal because the roads were poor. We went with a pile of files looking for individuals to interview, serve a summons, or make an arrest. Another constable and I often stayed overnight in an oil company bunkhouse. The center of the oilfield was 120 miles from Westlock, and if we made the trip in one day it was late before we returned. Perhaps the toughest day for me while in Westlock began with an investigation of a suicide at a farm about fifty miles west. I returned home for supper with Irene, and at about 8:00 P.M. a local doctor called to inform me of a fatal car accident some three miles west of town. I attended that accident scene until 1:00 A.M. with other members, and just as we were pulling into the detachment office one of the constables told me there was another accident about twenty-five miles south. That constable and I headed to that accident and returned home by 6:00 A.M.

To recount the events of that long day, the suicide was that of a man who had not been well and who ended his life by hanging himself from a rafter in a barn on his parents' farm. Interviews and written statements plus contacting the nearest coroner and arranging for removal of the body took most of the day. The accident in the evening near Westlock was quite sad. A couple and their infant child were injured, and one parent died at the scene. Written statements, photographs and measurements by the identification section from Edmonton, notification of next of kin, coroner, direction of traffic, and preservation of evidence for a subsequent inquest or trial were the usual requirements. This is what took until about 1:00 A.M.

The third sudden death investigation that day involved a hit and run driver. The deceased victim had been changing a tire on his car stopped at the edge of a two lane paved highway. The offending vehicle, traveling in the opposite direction of the stopped car, crossed over the centerline and struck the parked car, knocking the victim into the ditch where he died instantly. The offending vehicle was at the scene but the driver was nowhere to be found. I notified our detachment in Edmonton of the details and our suspicion that the offending driver somehow must have left the scene and headed south to Edmonton. While we were still at the accident scene, Edmonton detachment received a call from a man who had driven past the accident scene in his pickup truck, and when he arrived at his home in Edmonton a man who had apparently been riding in the back of his truck without his knowledge got out and started walking down the street. The Edmonton detachment was able to pick up the suspect a few blocks from the caller's house. Sufficient evidence to prove he was driving while intoxicated, as the prime cause of the accident, was not available. Ultimately however, this individual was convicted for leaving the scene of the accident.

On June 9, 1961, Irene, Eugene, and I moved to the small community of Andrew, Alberta, a town of some six hundred people in the midst of a rural farming area sixty miles northeast of Edmonton. The detachment office was attached to the living quarters consisting of a two-bedroom home with a fenced yard. It was a one-man detachment. Our second son, Michael, was born on November 6, 1961, a year and a half to the day after Eugene. He was born at the Lamont Hospital, some twenty-six miles from Andrew. On that occasion I had to be in Edmonton, and before returning to Lamont I stopped at Sacred Heart Church in Edmonton for a visit and to light a candle for Irene and our new baby. As it turned out, both with Eugene and Michael, I was in church when they were born! Doctors in those days were not amenable to having the husband in the delivery room. A one-man detachment required that I was on call virtually twenty-four hours a day, but I soon learned to sleep in when possible and to roll with the requirements of police duties. On January 23, 1963, Irene gave birth to twin girls, also at the Lamont Hospital. On that day it was quite cold and we followed the snowplow to the hospital. Upon arrival the doctor was waiting and I said, "I suppose I have to leave now?" to which he responded, "Would you like to stay?" When I jumped at the chance he had me put on a gown and mask and I was able to be in the delivery room when Veronica (6 lbs. 4 oz.) was born and some fifteen minutes later when Monica (5 lbs.) was born. This was a marvelous event, the miracle of life. I was so very proud of Irene and our daughters of course.

We were probably in the best situation to have three children in diapers. My office opened off the living room of our married quarters. I was able to help with the children. Irene and I took turns getting up at night with the girls, and I didn't have to get into the office until the morning chores were completed. Usually I bathed the girls each morning. We arranged for help from a woman who came in from time to time. Our two boys were growing and occasionally I would take them for a ride in the police car when I was just delivering a summons or getting the mail. This was a busy time for Irene and me and at times was quite difficult. After the girls were born, four of us would sit at the kitchen table while the twins, each in their plastic chairs similar to little car seats, sat on top of the chest-type deep freeze where they could oversee what was going on. I recall holding Irene and recounting the dream that Eugene Violini had shared with me: "I saw you in your uniform, close to your work, with several little children." This was comforting in the midst of our travail. It was comforting, too, to know that we were doing what we wanted to be doing and what appeared to be in accord with the will of God. We talked about this, realizing that many people never really arrive at what they believe to be their calling. We accepted our situation with gratitude.

Perhaps the most interesting case while in Andrew was that of the willful arson of a café in a nearby town. The part-time town policeman also served as fire chief and town foreman and oversaw municipal utilities. He called for assistance after the fire department had extinguished a fire in the café before it had completely demolished the building. It was possible to see where cloths had been strewn in the aisles between the booths, and even the seats of the booths had been cut and then gasoline poured on the cloths and the seats. Another thing that was noticeable was the fact that many of the dishes and accoutrements for running the café were missing. The provincial fire commissioner's office also participated in the investigation. During the course of my other duties, I received information that enabled me to obtain a search warrant to search the rural farm dwelling of a relative of the owner of the café. This search produced several boxes of dishes and utensils required for running a restaurant. Eventually I interviewed the owner who denied any involvement, however I went ahead with the charge of arson and a preliminary hearing was held with the result that the accused owner through his attorney acknowledged responsibility for starting the fire to defraud the insurance company.

In the spring of 1963 I was transferred to Bonnyville, a town of about five thousand, located 150 miles northeast of Edmonton. By my estimate, this community was then about 45 percent French, 30 percent Ukrainian, and the balance were native peoples both Treaty Indian and Métis (part Indian). The natives with Treaty Status came under the jurisdiction of the federal statute known as the Indian Act. The Métis people came under the jurisdiction of the provincial statute known as the Métis Betterment Act. Initially my family and I lived in an apartment located on the main street above the post office. It was hardly conducive to family living, and during my tenure in Bonnyville the Force initiated the construction of new detachment quarters built in a more residential area away from the commercial part of town. This was a wonderful improvement. On January 29, 1966, Irene gave birth to our son John, our fifth child. The detachment was a two-man contingent that soon became a three-man operation. There were two town policemen to carry out the local police responsibilities. Our responsibilities extended into the rural areas surrounding the town and included lakes, two or three of which were quite large and very popular for fishing and seasonal resort activities. Along with the addition of a third member came a second police car and a brand-new boat, motor, and trailer. We were responsible for enforcing the Small Vessel Regulations of the Canada Shipping Act, and when time would allow during peak periods we did endeavor to patrol Moose Lake, which was one of the larger more frequented lakes.

One of the purposes for our having a boat, besides preventative patrols, was to respond to accidental drownings. One very unfortunate and sad event that occurred was the death by drowning of an RCMP corporal, my former squad mate during training, and his friend who was a physician. Both were married men, and the wife of the corporal was expecting her fourth child at the time of this tragedy. As it happened both men had come to the detachment office while I was away on duty and told Irene that they would be at a particular cabin overnight and they invited me to socialize with them when I returned. I returned about 9 P.M. and decided not to join them. About 5 A.M. another corporal, who was part of the group at the lake cabin, came to the office and woke me. He described the events of their socializing and reported that about 2:00 A.M. the one corporal and the doctor went out in a boat to catch fish. The other corporal and another individual remained in the cabin playing cards. Time elapsed until finally the two in the cabin thought they would go out to see how the two fishermen were doing. It was then that they could see the boat capsized and noted the two men were missing. It was daylight by this time and it appeared quite certain the two men had drowned. A constable and myself went to the lake with the boat and dragging equipment, and we were able to recover the bodies of the two men.

Irene and I visited with the corporal's widow and subsequently attended the funeral, which was held in a large Orthodox church, because the Catholic church was too small. Two priests presided at the service, one was a brother of the deceased and the other was Father Duncan McDonnell who had been stationed at Sacred Heart Church in Edmonton when I attended there in 1958. He was then stationed at Clandonald, a small rural community, from where he had been called to officiate at this funeral. This event caused all of us in the Force to think about our mortality and, more important, to discuss how we would want to handle a family death were it to occur where we were posted. For our part, Irene and I decided that we would be buried from the church that we were then attending, as the location where we worshipped and where we were known. Despite our frequent moves, which proved to be especially difficult for Irene, we made the decision that our "temporary" homes were in fact "home"! I think this became our mindset because we didn't have extra help from family while we had our young children, and we knew and accepted that we had to cope on our own. Moreover, my role in the larger community and in the faith community required that we be "connected." I have since come to the deeper realization that one of the distinguishing theological principles of Catholicism is that of "communion" or "connectedness." Our initial family life was a kind of nomadic existence. It called us to a responsibility and an interest in the well-being of various communities, because of the motivation that we were doing what we (or at least I) wanted to do, confirmed as it were by Eugene Violini's prophetic dream suggesting that we were in sync with God's will.

In the summer of 1967 we were moved again, this time to Edmonton where I became a crime report reader in the "K" Division (provincial) Headquarters. I read police reports from all of the detachments in the province relating to traffic offences, both provincial and federal, plus all fraud and false pretence investigations. These reports had already been scrutinized at the sub/division level and upon my rereading were either sent back or referred to the provincial attorney general's office for further action, direction, or information. My role was to be a ghostwriter for the assistant Criminal Investigation Branch (CIB) officer, who was the person responsible for any necessary follow-up action. Although the procedure had proved to be foolproof over the years, it was quite bureaucratic and laborious. In the course of my tenure I felt the process could be streamlined to some extent and after about two years I was able to convince the CIB officer that we could modify the reporting procedure, and this in fact placed more responsibility at the detachment level. Part of my motivation was my recollection at having frequently sat up until 2 A.M. in the detachment office to type reports that essentially went nowhere except to sit on a shelf in the attorney general's office.

Probably my most interesting involvement at this level was to coordinate the investigation of a complex series of crimes. These were crimes involving fraud, false pretences, and stolen vehicles. The frequency and diverse areas of these similar crimes soon required that some singular coordination be brought to bear. I took over the files of some of the other readers and worked directly with the plainclothes member from the General Investigation Section (GIS) in Edmonton. It began to appear that the perpetrator either utilized a disguise or was very cunning in his methods. Information began to emerge that led us to connect through RCMP Headquarters with INTERPOL, the International Police Organization. This eventually resulted in a photograph from Scotland Yard of a Scottish male criminal who was bald. I had a friend in the hairdressing business from whom I obtained information about men's wigs, which I passed on to the local GIS investigator. He was able to locate a salon that catered to men wearing wigs, and upon showing the photograph they acknowledged that the individual was their customer and in fact was due to return to pick up a wig he had ordered. After staking out the location, the suspect was arrested and eventually received a substantial prison term, after which he was to undergo deportation proceedings.

My family and I lived in the south side of Edmonton in a rented home. This was in the Church of the Resurrection parish. I was active there with the Legion of Mary and as a leader of song both in that church and in the Church of St. Michael, which was twinned with Resurrection parish. We lived there the first year, until the owner decided to sell the home, which we were unable to purchase. We moved to the north part of Edmonton where we were able to buy a new three-bedroom condominium for a nominal down payment. We lived there for a little over a year until the summer of 1969 when we were transferred to Edson, 120 miles west of Edmonton. By that time, our eldest son Eugene had started school in Bonnyville. Michael started school at St. Bede's in south Edmonton where he and Eugene attended. When we moved to the north part of the city, Michael was in grade two at St. Dominic's and Eugene in grade three at the same school. Our parish was St. Anthony's, a Franciscan parish in conjunction with St. Anthony's College, a seminary prep school. I met with the pastor and started a group of the Legion of Mary at St. Anthony's while I was part of the curia level of the Legion of Mary in Edmonton.

In Edson, we once again occupied Government quarters in the RCMP building. During our stay there the RCMP entered a contract to take over policing of the town of Edson. This required renovating the RCMP building to accommodate more office space, and my family and I therefore moved out of the government quarters to private rented quarters. When we moved to Edson, Eugene went to one school, Michael to another. Eugene continued in the same school and Michael moved to another school. Two years later our twin daughters began school. In the first six months at Edson I attended five fatal motor vehicle accidents. The detachment consisted of three constables on rural work and four on highway patrol, with a corporal in charge of each unit. For the first time on a rural detachment we were allowed to hire a secretary. Previous to that all RCMP constables had to type their own reports. Upon entering the town contract, an additional five men came to Edson plus an additional rural constable. I was promoted to sergeant, and the member in charge of the town detail was a corporal as was the member in charge of the highway patrol. Ultimately we had two secretaries. We increased the number of police cars and included a four-wheel-drive vehicle to traverse isolated oil drilling and forestry access roads.

There were two or three investigations that stand out in my mind while I was in Edson. Two of the cases involved father/daughter incest, both of which occurred in rural locations and both men received substantial prison terms. In one case this was a second conviction with a different daughter, and in both instances the fathers returned to their families after serving their sentences. These were sad cases. I am not sure that the criminal justice system did anything to help these men or their families. The third case was a murder investigation that was reported early one Easter morning when I was expected to lead the choir at the 11:00 A.M. mass. The investigation was quite lengthy and lasted from about 5:00 A.M. until evening that Easter Sunday. It involved nontreaty native people in an isolated area during the course of a lengthy drinking bout. A woman had died after being beaten and dragged through a creek, and the evidence clearly supported a charge of aggravated assault, but because of the circumstances the prosecutor initiated a charge of murder. Eventually the charge was reduced because of insufficient evidence and a conviction was obtained for the assault.

The pastor of Sacred Heart parish in Edson was George Gunnip,

C.S.S.R, a former schoolteacher and a wonderful man. Eventually I began leading the singing from the front of the assembly. There was no Catholic school in Edson at the time, but George Gunnip maintained a great rapport with the local teachers and was able to have access to school facilities for after-hours religious education. I taught catechism to some high school students one year and I also served on the pastoral council for a year. When the detachment grew in size, some of the other members were Catholic. Sometimes I noticed the men were present and at other times I was too engrossed in the music to notice. The Force was a semi-military organization, and as the member in charge I was required to submit performance evaluations of the members. It is easy to see why, after a time, some of the men would tease me suggesting that I checked on their mass attendance while I was up at the front leading the singing. I didn't feel my involvement in the music ministry was a conflict, but it is possible the odd individual thought it was. The potential for being in a position of conflict was always present because of the public nature of my enforcement role in small communities.

During my stay in Edson, social changes began taking place. Substance abuse began to occur even in that small community, when previously it was confined to the major cities. When I asked the drug squad members to come to Edson to assist with enforcement, I was told, "Handle it yourself. We have more than we can handle here!" Because of the rural nature of the area, hippy communes emerged. In more than one instance draft dodgers from the United States lived in them and were a poor influence upon some of the local young people by introducing drug use and irresponsible lifestyles. We began to receive reports of adolescent runaways who would go to Toronto or Vancouver and get involved in the drug-infested areas of those cities and become lost to their families. Some young people managed to "fry their brains" as the expression went, because of substance abuse. The traditional means for dealing with drug use was arrest and imprisonment. Parents became alarmed and police came under scrutiny for how they were handling the problem. Our children were growing and I began to be concerned about how best to nurture family relationships. I remember asking a colleague from the drug squad whether he thought it best to tolerate some exposure of my children to the new social climate and the potential for substance abuse or to shelter them. Without hesitation his answer was "Shelter them!"

In July 1972 I was transferred to Edmonton. This was not a welcome transfer as far as my children were concerned. We had come to like

Edson and the children had many friends. My new role was in supervision, minor inspections, and investigations of complaints against the Force. After about a year my role changed again and involved "program evaluation" which was a new function that eventually became part of a new department called the Planning Branch. This was to be the area in which my final years in the Force were served. I took a variety of courses, was a part-time instructor on Planning and Practices of Management, and did a lot of administrative things influencing the Force to meet the demands of the many dimensions of change that were taking place in society. I began to serve in the capacity of the executive assistant to the Alberta Planning Board of the RCMP consisting of the four senior officers. For three years I compiled the planning documents that were forwarded to Ottawa for integration into the Federal Planning Programming and Budgeting process. A whole new world had opened up in my career with indications that I was being considered for a commissioned rank. Alberta was in an enviable position economically because of oil exploration in the face of the world energy crises and in particular because of the synthetic crude oil reserves of the tar sands in its northern regions.

Meanwhile my children were becoming adolescents. Irene continued, as we had agreed, as a stay-at-home mom. To her credit she continued to be present to the children when I was not, frequently staying up late even though I went to bed. Her comment was, "If I am not there for them when they come home, things they might share may never be shared." Our "several little children" soon were five teenagers, aged thirteen to nineteen. Mealtimes became bedlam. My demeanor, inherited and learned, was patriarchal, authoritative, and sometimes cynical. It was exacerbated by my policing experience and training, which in time can lead one to an attitude of suspicion and the view that there are no good people in the world. The common approach in criminal investigations is to look for the worst in people, to speculate on who might commit certain crimes, and in the course of our duties to order prisoners around. This behavior too easily spills over into family activities. Its effect upon Irene was to diminish her sense of self-esteem. Upon the children, to induce fear and, if it were to continue, disrespect or alienation. We learned this when we decided to take some self-improvement training to enhance family relationships. The whole new world that was opening up in my occupational pursuits needed to take place in my family. Irene and I were able to bring this about to some extent, and I think more than anything it was the providence of God that helped us to see the need and helped me to mellow and to allow a little more latitude in the activities of our children.

We lived in Sherwood Park, a large suburban area to the southeast of Edmonton. My two older sons had started playing hockey while in Edson, and since a large sports program existed in Sherwood Park, they were able to continue. John also began to participate. I took training to become a hockey referee and I was an active referee in the minor hockey program for about nine years. Working through the hockey executive, I developed an alternative process and remedial training for boys who incurred disciplinary action because of rule infractions such as fighting during hockey games. The motive was to discuss the infraction with the offender before the disciplinary committee and, rather than suspend, put the player back on the ice subject to his agreeing to undergo the remedial training. Being one of five boys, I had little insight into how to raise girls. It was always a concern of mine that my daughters received less of my time because of the emphasis on hockey and therefore of time spent with the boys. I tried to make up for this by attending other functions, but these were infrequent. One time I attended a tea with my daughters. Occasionally I attended their figure skating classes. Sometimes I drove them on their paper routes if the weather was especially cold. I attended their parent teacher sessions and most of their concerts. I think my daughters were good sports, because they attended many hockey games when probably they would have preferred other activities.

During this period, our children attended Catholic schools and eventually all went to Archbishop Jordan High School. Religion classes had sustained a distinct loss and an inconsistency in the aftermath of the Second Vatican Council. Former curriculums for religion classes were abandoned. New curriculums were experimental, sometimes shallow, and teachers were apprehensive and unsure. I got together with several parents and headed a committee to support the teachers who were required to teach religion to the students. We met about once a month for dialogue with those teachers, who received us well and shared what they were attempting to do in their religion classes. They accepted suggestions from our group, and I think we served as a buffer during a time of major change. If we did nothing else, the teachers became aware that we were interested in our faith and we supported their efforts to transmit the essence of that faith, in the midst of the changes that were taking place. Our methodology was largely the concept of management by objectives with which I had become familiar in my work. An essential aspect of that process is "participative management." We sought to identify and develop "results" or "outcomes" on which the parents and the teachers were in agreement. It is a wonderful vehicle because the individuals who participate become invested in the outcome and more motivated to seeing the purposes achieved. It was a method of consultation for corporations as well as for government to enhance productivity and morale, a concept that was espoused by the Second Vatican Council for "consultative" bodies in the church working with pastors and bishops, even though we weren't fully aware of that at the time.

8

OFFICIAL CHANGES MADE TO THE PRIESTHOOD

> Celibacy is not required by the nature of priesthood itself.
> Decree on the Ministry and Life of Priests

The celibate tradition and its initiating "law" from the Second Lateran Council has continued to this day. The priesthood underwent changes over the centuries, which influenced the priesthood that we have come to know in our day. There were periods when, because of nepotism and other influences, men were ordained whose motives were not what was required of priests. A notable renewal was the seminary training and educational requirements that evolved and continued essentially to the present time. Over and above such historic renewal movements, there have been relatively recent changes made with respect to the Catholic priesthood or the sacrament of holy orders.

Two documents promulgated under Pope Paul VI which have a bearing on the 1139 rule of celibacy are the Decree on the Ministry and Life of Priests (December 7, 1965)[1] and the encyclical on priestly celibacy *Sacerdotalis Caelibatus* (June 24, 1967).[2] Both documents made it quite clear that celibacy is not required by the nature of priesthood itself. Following these formal pronouncements, the following reform of orders was made:

- In *Sacrum Diaconatus Ordinem* (June 18, 1968), Pope Paul VI re-established the permanent diaconate and eliminated the impediment of marriage for permanent deacons. In many dioceses in the

United States where training exists for married deacons, the wives of these candidates accompany them throughout the training which takes place over a two or three year period.

- A further review of celibacy was discussed during the Second General Assembly of the Synod of Bishops in 1971. The Holy Father and the bishops who were present considered the possibility of ordaining married men "of mature age and proven life." At that time more than half of the world's bishops present for the voting considered the ordination of married men to be a pastoral necessity. This information was reported following the synod under the title "The Ministerial Priesthood." However no action has been taken and celibacy remains a mandatory condition for priesthood in the Western church.

The following further changes were made in relation to orders:

- In *Ministeria Quaedam* (August 15, 1972), Pope Paul VI eliminated first tonsure, changed the minor orders to ministries, and divided the function of the subdiaconate between the two ministries of lector and acolyte.[3] Previous to this there were seven orders in holy orders. These consisted of porter, lector, acolyte, exorcist, subdeacon, deacon, and presbyter. In retrospect this was a major change to the ministry of the ordained. Today candidates for the priesthood are enrolled in the ministries of lector and acolyte and ordained as transitory deacons as distinguished from permanent deacons, and then as presbyters (or priests).
- Pope John Paul II (June 1980) sanctioned exceptions to the rule of celibacy granting the sacrament of orders to married former male Episcopal clergy in the United States.[4] The exception granted to Episcopal clergy has since expanded to include former clergymen of other Christian denominations in other countries who have since been ordained to the Roman Catholic priesthood while married.

This change to our priestly tradition was initiated as a kind of "affirmative action," an ecumenical gesture granting a privilege to the person converting to Catholicism. As with any affirmative action, it generated a reverse discrimination affecting married Catholic men who perceive a calling to the ordained ministry. In the view of many celibate clerics it is a double standard. In the United States there are approximately one hundred ordained and functioning married Roman Catholic priests.

Beyond these formal changes, a more subtle but greater change has impacted the Catholic priesthood. It has its origins in three documents: (1) *Lumen Gentium*—the Dogmatic Constitution on the Church,[5] (2) *Sacrosanctum Concilium*—the Constitution on the Sacred Liturgy,[6] and (3) *Apostolicam Actuositatem*—the Decree on the Apostolate of the Laity.[7] The heavy stress in the former tradition on the hierarchical nature of the church and on the perception of ministry as fundamentally clerical and sacramental have been modified by the ecclesiology of the Second Vatican Council. That council contextualized the teaching on the hierarchy by understanding the church as a community of God's people (*Lumen Gentium*, 11). The former tradition was recorded in the 1566 Catechism of the Catholic Church and the 1917 Code of Canon Law. After the council it took a number of years, but the updated theology and pastoral changes from the three mentioned conciliar documents are now reflected in the 1983 revised Code of Canon Law and the 1992 revised Catechism of the Catholic Church.

These major documents were not revised without a great deal of follow-up and study in order to incorporate the changes into the theological, pastoral, and ecclesial context that would impact the Sacrament of Holy Orders. Work to revise the first document began in 1963 when Pope John XXIII established the pontifical commission for the revision of the Code of Canon Law. Paul VI enlarged its membership in 1964 and it began its formal work in 1965. Initially there were ten study groups and these were increased to sixteen in 1967. The revision of the Code of Canon Law therefore took virtually twenty years.

In 1986 Pope John Paul II commissioned twelve cardinals and bishops chaired by Cardinal Ratzinger to prepare a draft of the new catechism, the second major document. An editorial committee of seven diocesan bishops assisted them. Nine subsequent drafts were edited and Pope John Paul II approved the new catechism on October 11, 1992, after six years of preparation, and twenty-seven years after the council that dramatically influenced its content.

The council saw ministry as rooted in baptism, making it a vocational responsibility of all God's people and not just the ordained. Essentially this initiated a shift to *the priesthood of all the baptized*. We are all baptized priest, prophet, and king, and since the Vatican II renewal, we rightfully ask: "How am I priest? How am I prophet? How am I king (or servant leader)?" Ordained clerics too began to question: "If there is a priesthood of all the baptized, what is the role of the ordained?" As a result of all of these changes, practice within the church is still struggling to catch up, to understand, and to fully assimilate the changes. What I had learned during my seminary studies is that this is about different job descriptions. It does not all start with the ministry of the ordained, which is one job description. This does not denigrate the role of the priest, rather it identifies the responsibility inherent in the universal priesthood of all the baptized that needs to be embraced more appropriately.

These official changes made to the priesthood had far-reaching implications. Almost thirty-five years after the council, efforts are still being made to answer the question: "What is a priest?" There is still a struggle to work out the distinctions of ordained episcopacy and priesthood in relation to the priesthood of all the baptized, as described by Monsignor Philip J. Murnion, director of the National Pastoral Life Center in New York City.[8] I believe, as will be seen in later chapters, that this book offers hope for the contemporary church to unravel the major dysfunction that is inhibiting this struggle and in effect has distorted ordained episcopacy and priesthood in the church. The ordained, in effect, are powerless to resolve this dilemma alone.

9

MY SECOND CAREER

*The grass withers, the flower fades;
But the word of our God will stand forever.*
                                    Isaiah 40: 8

In 1975, the commanding officer of "K" Division asked me if I would accept a commission in the Force. I said that I would like to discuss this with my wife and asked if I could get back to him. He was very gracious and agreed. At that time a regular member could take a pension after twenty years, ideally twenty-five years. Once appointed to a commission a member's pension plan changed, and he had to remain for the full thirty-five years of service and could be transferred anywhere in Canada. Salary and pension benefits were changed and certainly increased. I discussed this briefly with Irene and she consented so I told the commanding officer I would accept the promotion. Within two or three weeks, the commanding officer informed me that procedures were changing, and they would be introducing a board before which I would have to appear after writing a paper as a kind of thesis on a subject of my choice. I agreed to follow the procedure that was being established.

Soon I received information about the new procedure, and I decided to write about the planning process in the Force. A couple of individual members who knew me told me it would be a cinch because nobody else knew much about the planning process. The paper was a good exercise and when all was ready I appeared before the board consisting of three commissioned officers, one of whom I knew quite well, the other two only by reputation. The dialogue was quite thorough and the board members asked me many questions about administrative issues and my views about the recently initiated overtime provision, the Staff Relations Representative program that had been instituted a year or two before, and the system of non-commissioned officer messes and the officers mess. Because I had been involved in evaluating programs and in instructing on management practices in the Force, my answers were somewhat radical, and clearly the three interviewers, who had limited personnel training or interviewing skills beyond police interrogation methods, interpreted my responses quite negatively.

In retrospect, I was naïve to think that the board members would be looking for aspiring officer candidates with creative initiative and relative confidence to adapt enforcement methods and administrative practices that would keep pace with the changing social conditions of the time. What was actually happening was that the three interviewers were evaluating me to determine how well I would conform to the military discipline and protocol to which they were accustomed as commissioned officers. The board opted to defer me for one year, and their written comments stated that they found my views disloyal to the commissioner. The principal issue under discussion was the Staff Relations Representative program designed to provide a vehicle for members with a grievance. The grievance would be referred to the commissioner of the Force through a Staff Relation member. The procedure had some merit, but once a decision was rendered it provided for a further appeal by the member to the commissioner. My suggestion to the board was that the program did not allow for a completely objective appeal process such as other agencies in the Federal Public Service enjoyed. An independent review board heard their appeals, whereas a grievance appeal of the commissioner's decision for members of the Force would go back to the commissioner. The board's decision was disappointing to me and to others with whom I worked, but it was an awakening for me and caused me to reassess my career and the desirability of becoming a commissioned officer like the men who interviewed me.

The pressure to conform at the senior levels of the Force was all-encompassing, and the role to which I had aspired lost some luster in my estimation. There was a stereotypical authoritarianism that at certain times and certain places would have to take precedence. What came to my mind was the nickname that the rank and file members dubbed the Officers Indoctrination Course. They called it the "hate course." It was a pause that gave Irene and me additional time for reflection. Irene was always able to communicate and she did so during this time. Irene was more of a private person than I was, and the constant moves had already taken their toll on her desire to establish a permanent home. The thought that she would have to accompany me on official functions and perhaps have to entertain for political or governmental purposes seemed threatening to her. At about this time the three senior officers in Alberta who knew me and had confidence in me went to pension. Three senior level officers, one who had a reputation as the toughest autocrat on the Force, succeeded them. I attended a function where this new senior officer was guest speaker and I thought, "If I stay I will end up being like him!" Several factors converged in my mind, including the issue of limited salary, a desire to better provide for my family, and in particular a desire to respect Irene's point of view. It was a difficult decision for me, but once I decided that a commission was out—that I no longer aspired to go as far as I could in the Force—I resigned.

The next few years were a challenge and a time of continued learning. My immediate activity was in commission sales. After a few months, I applied to become the manager of an industry association where I learned about land use planning and development agreements for residential land development. In March of 1979, after two and a half years as the industry association manager, I became a district manager for a member company that was a major land developer in western Canada. I continued to learn and began to feel more settled in what I was doing. Meanwhile I continued to referee hockey and to adapt to life outside the Force. It was a big adjustment for me, because the Force and my remaining in the Force had been my main focus. Just as I had dreamt of wearing the RCMP uniform when our family first moved to California in 1952, I found myself dreaming that I was still in the Force and wearing the uniform. With self-improvement courses and much self-affirmation, I managed to release and let go of my tense hold on the Force.

In 1981 an opportunity arose when the company planned to start a new region in Red Deer. I had been working that area from Edmonton and the opportunity was quite attractive, but my having left the Force to establish a permanent home was the first hurdle to be considered. About this time Irene underwent a hysterectomy to correct a condition of endometriosis from which she had suffered for several years. Irene agreed to the move to Red Deer as long as our daughters and youngest son would move with us, as our two eldest sons by that time had opted to remain in Sherwood Park. Red Deer was a smaller community of approximately

55,000 people whereas Edmonton's population at that time exceeded 500,000. John would continue his schooling in Red Deer, and our daughters thought they would work for a year before going to college. Ultimately, the company selected me and I was promoted to regional manager, and so we moved to Red Deer where I opened the company's land development office. We managed to sell our home in Sherwood Park and had a new home built for us by the housing division of our company in Red Deer.

When we first settled in Red Deer, we attended both of the two churches there. I remember in particular when at St. Mary's Church our daughter Monica heard a homily that was particularly demeaning to women. She was so upset over it that she went to see the priest after mass and gave him a piece of her mind. After that we began to attend and became parishioners of Sacred Heart Church. Monica worked in a bank and Veronica worked as an aide in a large home for people with mental disabilities. This was a difficult role for her. One day at the supper table I noticed that Veronica had a bruise on her face, and when I asked about it she became emotional and told me of an incident in the behavioral management unit where one of the residents struck her with his fist. Monica and Veronica remained in Red Deer for about a year, and then went back to Edmonton to attend college. We helped them to become established in an apartment they shared with another girlfriend and former classmate. John was then our only child remaining at home.

After the first year in Red Deer, we experienced an economic recession, during which all employees received a reduced income and the company pulled together to renegotiate agreements and to survive in that period of minimal sales and high interest rates. Slowly we succeeded and the economy began to pick up. Sales and development activity likewise picked up. Our company managed to acquire a significant parcel of land on which I was able to oversee the development of a high-quality residential subdivision. During these years, Irene's father passed away, and in a few months her mother came to stay with us. Her mother was still grieving and had contracted diabetes. It was most appropriate that she stay with us. We had room and we were happy to have her. We began to learn about diabetes, insulin use, and blood-sugar-level testing.

When we first began attending Sacred Heart Church, the choir was still singing from the choir loft at the back of the church, the music was pre–Vatican II in content, and the assembly did not participate in singing. A new pastor arrived about the same time as my family and I. He was

Karl Raab, whom I had known in Edmonton while he was rector of St. Joseph's Seminary, and with whom I had served on a Vocations Team representing the Knights of Columbus. Eventually I asked Karl how long he was going to put up with the pre–Vatican II form of worship. Our parish in Sherwood Park had long since changed to the post–Vatican II liturgies, and and the Red Deer parish was clearly behind the times. The previous pastor had not entertained a great many changes during his eleven-year tenure despite the fact the Vatican Council had ended in 1965. Karl acknowledged my impatience but insisted that any change should take place with caution, since the priest in a town some fifty miles distant had pressed the choir to come to the front to lead the singing and the choir all came down, sat in the front pews with their arms folded, and quit singing!

Soon after Karl arrived, a new assistant in the person of Sister Bernadette O'Neil arrived to work at Sacred Heart Church in Red Deer. Sister Bernie, as we called her, was very much a Vatican II Catholic. At times her work encountered resistance and I would challenge her views. For the most part however, Bernie was a prophet and, in retrospect, she was my teacher.

I started singing with the choir in the loft more or less to become familiar with the members and their repertoire. In time, people in Sacred Heart parish encouraged me to start leading the singing from the front. I tried to work through the parish council and the pastor, and eventually the pastor and I attended a choir practice and spoke to the choir about the idea of change. It was agreed that I would lead the assembly from the front with the choir remaining in the loft with their director, who would gesture broadly to the choir so that I could follow his lead when leading the assembly. This seemed like overkill to me, but there was grumbling among the choir and one man said that the day that the choir moved downstairs would be the day he would go to St. Mary's Parish! I made a visit to this man's home and did my best to assure him his wonderful tenor voice was a gift and would greatly assist the community. In spite of my pleading, he was adamant. He would leave if we moved the organ to the front. He had a daughter who was an aspiring organist, and she sometimes played the organ when the regular organist was not available.

This song-leading procedure was quite cumbersome and did not work very well, since there was always a second or two lapse for the sound to reach the front of the church where I was standing. We made do this way for about three months, until one day the regular choir director called the substitute director at the last minute to stand in for him. The singing at that mass did not go well, and the substitute director was quite incensed and decided to quit. Eventually another meeting was held with the pastor and me, and the outcome was that we would look into the idea of moving the organ to the front of the church and eventually the choir would move to the front. I visited the substitute director who informed me that the regular choir director had resigned and the substitute director declined to assist in any way. A smaller organ was donated and was installed in the sanctuary.

The young woman organist, daughter of the disgruntled tenor, who was quite traditional in her faith because of the influence of her father, felt that it was sinful for her to be sitting at the edge of the sanctuary accompanying me for the early Sunday mass. I did my best to persuade her to continue and she did so reluctantly for a few weeks. Eventually a representative of an organ company came by and offered to install an organ without obligation to see if we liked the new electronic instrument. We jumped at the chance and the choir for the 11 A.M. Sunday mass found a new home nearer the front of the church beside that organ.

Although we did not buy the organ and later moved the existing organ down from the choir loft, it did facilitate the much-needed change. When I led the singing in church, Irene would sit near the front and affirmed me by her demeanor and comments. For quite a while Irene and the pastor and the faithful choir members were the only ones to offer positive feedback. A couple of years after this change in the liturgical music, the assembly had begun to participate reasonably well and much new music had been introduced. I was leaving church after the 11:00 A.M. Sunday mass, when a woman stopped me and told me that she had been one of the former choir members that had resisted the change. She explained that she was a convert to Catholicism and at first didn't understand, but that particular Sunday had been especially moving for her and she now understood and she wanted to thank me. That was the most meaningful feedback that I received.

Despite Irene's shyness, sometimes when she knew the people involved she would seize an opportunity to accompany me in some activity. On one occasion Irene and I visited and brought Holy Communion to the wife of a former RCMP colleague who was suffering from ovarian cancer. We didn't know at the time that Irene had the same cancer growing in her.

In December of 1984, Irene became ill and in telling me about it she related that she was experiencing pain similar to that which she experienced prior to her hysterectomy. This was scary. A doctor's examination revealed an abnormal growth and resulted in a return visit to the gynecologist in Edmonton, who instructed that Irene undergo surgery as soon as possible. Irene decided to have the surgery in Red Deer. Arrangements were made for her to have a laparoscopy and a biopsy preliminary to surgery. As it turned out, I was leading the singing at the funeral liturgy for my former colleague's wife at the very same time that Irene was undergoing an exploratory surgical procedure that confirmed her disease. My thoughts and prayers were for Irene in the midst of the funeral liturgy. When I rushed home after the funeral, Irene's mother told me the doctor had called. I called him and he confirmed that Irene had a malignant ovarian tumor and that they set her surgery for the next day. I went back to Irene's mother who was in bed upstairs in our home, and together we cried before I went to see Irene. I then went to the day surgery area of the Red Deer Hospital and visited with Irene. She was quite matter of fact. When I discussed the possibility of her waking up from the anticipated surgery with a colostomy, Irene stated she would rather die than have to experience that.

A team of doctors performed the surgery on Irene, and the report to me was that they had removed the entire tumor except a portion that was a centimeter in size. Chemotherapy was recommended and the oncologist prescribed heavy doses on a weekly basis, with Irene being part of a treatment study of similar cases from Edmonton to Boston. These treatments were very difficult. The chemotherapy was administered intravenously over a period of about three hours. Usually I stayed with Irene and had a sandwich with her. Most of the time she could not eat much. Our twenty-fifth wedding anniversary was spent in this way, eating a sandwich! When we left the hospital clinic where the treatments were administered, Irene was nauseous and had to vomit in a plastic bag before we reached home. She went to bed immediately and slept for a few hours and then managed to eat some porridge and began feeling the effects of the chemo, which barely wore off before she had another treatment. Irene lost her hair.

We needed help to manage the household while I continued to manage the development activities. Ironically, her mother rose to the occasion, seemingly recovering from her ailments out of need, and took over cooking and cleaning, thus enabling Irene to cope with her treatment. After about three months of this aggressive treatment, Irene told the doctor: "I would rather die than take any more chemotherapy." I supported her and

Irene stopped taking the treatments. We began to research and try all manner of vitamin therapy and any natural means that would be beneficial. Irene's hair grew back more curly, and we had a good year, during which we attended aerobic classes and did a number of things together. This was one of the best periods of our marriage. After a few months, Irene's mother left to visit another daughter, and while there she had a mild stroke after which she was moved to an extended-care home in Calgary.

In 1985, my mother who had been living in Kamloops passed away. My brother Bob and I went to Kamloops and attended to the necessary estate concerns, then arranged for her body to be transported to Winnipeg, Manitoba, for the funeral. My four brothers and I were together in Winnipeg for the funeral, where we all had a hand in planning the event and where we met with our relatives there. Mother was buried in the cemetery of the Belgian Church of the Sacred Heart in St. Boniface. Mother had been a widow for thirty years and never remarried. She raised her last three sons as a single parent and in her latter working years in California she was a priest's housekeeper.

In the latter part of 1986, Irene began to falter in what had appeared to be a period of remission. At first it was too difficult for her to attend the aerobic classes so she stopped them. Gradually, I encouraged her to go back to the doctor to make sure. Irene didn't want to but finally consented. When we saw the oncologist again, he let us know that our efforts were to no avail and vitamins were not the answer. We came to realize the period of recovery that Irene had experienced was due primarily to the chemotherapy. The tumor had returned and over time Irene was able to notice that one chemotherapy treatment actually would shrink the tumor. She knew that as much as she didn't like the chemo she needed it. However, the doctor agreed that Irene would only receive the treatment about every three weeks, which she was willing and able to tolerate. Eventually Irene became weaker and the disease was spreading. On two or three occasions Irene was admitted to the hospital for treatment. On the advice of the Red Deer Clinic, Irene was treated for about ten days in the Cross Cancer Clinic in Edmonton, where I learned how to administer total parenterol nutrition intravenously and to administer pain medication subcutaneously. The nutritional fluids and pain medications were delivered to the house. Irene was able to stay at home where we had a hospital bed in the main floor family room and were assisted by a home care nurse.

During the period of Irene's illness, a change of pastors occurred. The new pastor was Duncan MacDonnell. He was very supportive during Irene's illness. I had continued as a song leader and volunteer director of music for the parish and Duncan was my friend. He visited Irene in the hospital on one occasion while I was present. When Irene was at home on total parenterol nutrition, our son John was able to be there until noon but then he went to work. I spoke with Duncan and asked if it would be possible for some of the prayer group to be with Irene after lunch until about 5 P.M. when I was at work. He arranged with several members of the prayer group to take turns, and he himself was the first one to stay with Irene. Later one of the sisters came and stayed and eventually several people, among them some who did voluntary housework for me. All of them were just wonderful, and I was especially pleased for Irene for whom this was very comforting. For me it was a real blessing.

The last seven weeks of Irene's life were spent at home, except for a further surgical procedure to insert an abdominal drainage tube. The circumstances surrounding the insertion of the drainage tube were challenging. It was a Sunday morning when I was to lead the singing at the 9:00 A.M. mass. As was our practice, Irene had received the 2500 cc's of liquid nutrition during the night, and I removed the apparatus in the morning and was carrying out the aseptic procedure to inject a solution to counter any clotting when we observed fluid leaking from under the bandage covering the draining-tube incision. I asked Irene what she thought we should do, and she suggested lifting the bandage to see what was happening, and when I did this fluid began leaking much more quickly and we had to use paper towels. Clearly we needed to take Irene back to the hospital to deal with this. I managed to call Duncan to let him know I wouldn't be able to lead the singing, and he was very empathetic and told me to do what I had to do. The ambulance transported Irene and me. The doctor who had inserted the drainage tube was in the hospital, and he attended to her quite quickly after our arrival. He decided that what had happened was the drainage tube was not receiving the fluid, and so he simply attached an ostomy bag to collect the abdominal fluid and Irene returned home. This meant that among the nursing chores I then had to empty the ostomy bag.

One occasion stands out in my mind during these last weeks when Irene was at home and I was her primary caregiver. I had to attend a practice with the young man who had begun playing the organ. I arranged for

Irene to have the telephone right beside her bed and told her I would be at the church until 9:00 P.M., but I would hurry right home. This was acceptable to Irene and so off I went about 7:15 P.M., and the organist and I went through all the music. The next thing I knew it was about 9:20 P.M. I told him I had to go. I hadn't realized it was so late. All I could think of was Irene's situation. I gathered up my music things, and as I was rushing out of the church through a hallway past the sacristy door, words came into my mind, clearly and unmistakably, "Aren't you going to bring me to Irene?" This was amazing to me, but in the midst of my haste I automatically responded. Knowing how to gain access to the sacristy and the tabernacle, I hurriedly grabbed a pix, went to the tabernacle for the Eucharist, put the key back, and hurried home. When I arrived Irene was fine and confirmed that she had had no difficulties. I told her what had happened and how it was as if Jesus had spoken to me when I was rushing past the sacristy. Irene understood and together we received the Eucharist in the confidence and love of our God whom we trusted and whom we knew was supporting us in the midst of our struggle.

Those weeks and the anxiety associated with them were difficult times, but they were among the most meaningful of my life and, despite the sickness and disutility which Irene experienced, I believe they were very meaningful for her too. One time close to the end of her life it seemed to me that Irene was becoming a little distant. I was attending to her evening nutritional feeding and Irene was looking off to the side and wasn't communicating. I suppose this made me wonder if Irene wasn't happy with me or if I had displeased her, so I asked her, "Do you love me?" Immediately, Irene seemed to come back into relation with me and she said, "Oh yes, I love you very, very much!"

10

THE ORDAINED PRIESTHOOD IN CRISES

> They tie up heavy burdens, hard to bear, and lay them on the shoulders of others; but they themselves are unwilling to lift a finger to move them.
>
> Matthew 23:4

The major documents of the Second Vatican Council brought about significant changes in the life and practices of the church. The subsequent changes made to the priesthood under Pope Paul VI and Pope John Paul II listed in chapter 8 added to the impact of those changes. These significant changes in the church's life took their toll on the lay people as well as on the ordained.

The postconciliar encyclical *Humanae Vitae* (On Human Life, 1968) of Pope Paul VI that in effect forbade universal use of "the pill" by married couples searching for a way to be faithful to the "natural law" teaching concerning the transmission of life was in many ways as difficult for priests to deal with as for the laity. An untold number of priests left their ministry because they could not reconcile this new teaching with the struggles of conscience faced by many couples with whom they ministered. I know this firsthand because a former priest working as a management consultant on a study for the RCMP told me this was why he left his priestly ministry and he knew of others who left for the same reason. There is no way to measure the numbers adversely impacted by this teaching. Certainly the well-known theologian Father Charles Curran who sought a reconsideration of this teaching by the church was "adversely impacted," having been barred from teaching in a Catholic university.

The document on the church that gave a new emphasis to the people of God as the priesthood of all the baptized created a crisis of identity among the ordained. It gave rise to the thought: "If every Catholic is a priest, what am I?" Many celibate clerics have remained faithful throughout this unprecedented time of transition. However, numerous clerics left active ministry. In the United States alone, some eight thousand priests left their public ministry between 1966 and 1972.[1] During the pontificate of Pope Paul VI (d. 1978), approximately 32,000 priests worldwide were laicized, that is, relieved of their office and from the obligation of celibacy. After the accession of Pope John Paul II, more than ten thousand petitions for laicization were put on hold.[2] It is estimated that more than one hundred thousand priests have left active ministry since the council. Another source estimated that by 2002 there would be more nonfunctioning priests in the United States than active functioning priests.

In 1980 in Edmonton when I participated in planning for a new church building, it was necessary to ignore the ideal size of a worship space that would accommodate approximately three hundred people, and instead design a new building that could accommodate twelve hundred to fifteen hundred people—principally because of the shortage of ordained priests. I didn't really understand this at the time. For the past several years, dioceses have been holding meetings and having discussions to develop strategies to consolidate, close, or link parishes in anticipation of fewer priests.

The principle crisis that has evolved in the ordained priesthood is *a shortage of celibate males*. Young men today are no longer willing to give fifty years of celibate living. This ought to lead to the real cause. Unfortunately, it eludes those having authority for its remedy. This crisis emanates from one root cause. That cause is *power that oppresses* from whatever level it operates. I make this claim after studying for the priesthood for four years and subsequently serving as a professional lay ecclesial minister for more than eight years in two parishes in the Archdiocese of Seattle. If we were to look upon this oppression as a disease afflicting the church, even one crisis ought to be a turning point. Unfortunately, this oppression is intractably entrenched to the point that several crises have emerged. This chapter focuses on the crises that impact the ordained priesthood. The ordained priesthood does not exist for its individual priests. It exists to serve the people of God. It therefore becomes apparent that these crises affecting the ordained priesthood impact the universal priesthood of all the baptized.

A second crisis in the ordained priesthood is the **sexual abuse of minors.** I first became aware of this during my police career in the early 1970s when other policemen told me of incidents that I took to be quite isolated since there was little public knowledge of them. In 1983 Sister Bernadette O'Neil serving in my parish in Red Deer expressed her concern to me without offering specific incidents. In 1989, acting on the public revelation of sexual abuse perpetrated by religious and clerics in Newfoundland, Archbishop Penny established a commission of inquiry chaired by Gordon Winter. The revelations involved numerous incidents of pedophilia as well as homosexuality, and criminal charges implicated a number of clerics. The Winter Report was issued in June 1990, excerpts of which were sent to me by the Archdiocese of Edmonton for which I was studying at the time. It is significant that the commission had this to say:

> The Commission heard many calls for, and no opposition to, the notion of a married Clergy as an option for those who find that they have not received what canon law refers to as the "gift" of celibacy, and who find celibacy of no value to their priestly ministry.[3]
> ... The Commission therefore concludes that celibacy as an absolute requirement for the ministerial priesthood must be more fully examined by bishops and that for some individuals it may create excessive and destructive pressures [4]. ...
> ... [Recommendation 54] that the Archbishop join with other bishops across Canada to address fully, directly, honestly and without reservation questions relating to the problematic link between celibacy and the ministerial priesthood.[5]

After the Winter Report was released Archbishop Penny resigned. I am not aware of any public acknowledgement by the Vatican or the Canadian bishops that they would more fully examine celibacy as an absolute requirement for ministerial priesthood. I do know that policies have been adopted in most Canadian dioceses to handle complaints of abuse by clerics. Although Archbishop Penny tendered his resignation, he remained in office for six months until the Vatican accepted it, even though this was the culmination of a report commissioned by the archbishop and followed two years of extensive, horrific media coverage. This was insulting to the people of Newfoundland.[6] In my view it was also oppressive of the archbishop because it did not accept the integrity of his stepping down. Since that time I have read about many similar scandals and monetary settlements in other countries. I wonder about the role of bishops in the face of these scandals and costly settlements. I don't mean simply making a policy in a diocese. I am referring to the governance of the universal church by the college of bishops in unity with the pope. I will enlarge on this later in this chapter.

Archbishop Penny accepted the blame, as it were, but in my view the entire scandal and his loss to the church were manifestations of codependency to institutional oppression. The Winter Report's reference to "what canon law refers to as the 'gift' of celibacy" has gone nowhere. Clearly, it is not a "gift" when it is imposed. Authoritarian rule over the bishops of the world seems to preclude episcopal leadership. Worse yet, the universal college of bishops has acquiesced in a conspiracy of silence. The Winter Report was laid to rest. Are these not signs of the times that are being ignored?

On one of my seminary breaks in 1989, I had occasion to visit a priest in the forensic unit of the Alberta Hospital in Edmonton where he was serving a sentence for sexually abusing children. My visit arose out of concern for him. I had often visited incarcerated people, and since I had worshipped with this man it was the least I could do. I understood the conditions under which he had been laboring in the "vineyard," for I had worked in rural, semi-primitive, and isolated areas during my police career. I was impressed by the treatment the priest had been receiving to correct his "deviancy." But I wondered how much the "imposed" condition of mandatory celibacy affected this man's actions in the context of the environment in which he was working.

By the "context of the environment" I refer to the cultures of origin, the economic disparities of the priest and the children, the leadership responsibility of the priest and the vulnerability of the children, and the effect of the deprivation of sexual intimacy on this lonely man driving to rural semi-isolated locations year after year to teach and preach about a loving unseen deity to people, especially children, who were trusting and affectionate. Just thinking about the environment again reminds me of the impoverished people there. Many families were without running water and used to drive to town to launder their clothes. I remember this priest pedophile telling me some of the details of his offence. His need and ability to talk about his deviancy were part of the treatment he was receiving. Where he is now and whether the church is still carrying out the responsibility for his continued support pursuant to his incardination (attachment to a diocese) I do not know.

In 1990, while I was still in the seminary, I discussed priest pedophilia with a visiting former seminarian who was a trained social worker before becoming a priest. He became chancellor of a diocese and shared with me some of his involvement with and understandings of pedophilia. During my police career some thirty years earlier, I had been given to understand that pedophilia was considered incurable. This was the position of two psychiatrists who were called to give evidence at the trial of a pedophile defendant at which I was also a witness. In their view little could be done to rehabilitate a pedophile. Their comment, which I will never forget, was "You may as well throw away the key." From a Christian point of view, we simply do not write off another human being. I believe that medical science has since developed ways of helping pedophiles, but our Christian responsibilities do require us not to jeopardize the safety of others, hence keeping pedophiles away from children continues to be essential.

Some people argue that pedophilia and priestly celibacy are not related. However, I believe there is a relationship. It is a "systemic" relationship. It is a product of the institutional oppression that needs to be understood. The predominantly white male celibate hierarchical system that characterizes Roman Catholicism is at the heart of these crises in the priesthood. The public outcry over the abuse of children by priests brought this crisis forward. These abuses and the cover-ups by bishops have been devastating to the victims, to faithful clerics, to Catholics worldwide, and to the way in which non-Christians perceive Catholicism. Meanwhile, crises in the ordained priesthood become more acute with every passing year as the numbers of priests diminish and membership in the church increases. Most of the ministry in the church today is carried out by the nonordained. The church in the United States is growing by approximately a hundred thousand new members each year through the Rite of Christian Initiation of Adults (RCIA). The following passage brings a sharper focus:

> ... [T]he sexual problematic for Catholicism is a function of its acting as an Institution does rather than as a Church should, so that its bureaucratic attentions infect what its pastoral possibilities would otherwise heal. This bureaucracy is a shadow Church that reflects less the glory of God than the cunning of the world, less a sense of eternity than of drowning in time. As an institution, its chief goal is to perpetuate itself—for it is threatened more by time than by eternity.
>
> This shadow Church keeps itself together as an Institution by investing its power in keeping its members in a frightened and depen-

dent state. Wise in the world's ways and friendly with the Mammon of Iniquity, the Institution knows that if it can control sexuality, it can maintain its mastery over human beings. This emphasis on power diminishes its true authority to help ordinary men and women put away childish things and grow up even by small steps, the way we learn to walk and talk—the way, imperfect but tolerant of failings, we become human.[7]

To support my contention that there is a connection between pedophilia and celibate priests, it is necessary to recall the historic respect accorded Catholic priests. The earliest, albeit questionable, mindset discussed in chapter 2 was that a person could not be holy if he or she was sexually active (even in marriage). In the second millennium, the "enforced innocence" of the 1139 law of celibacy ensured that priests would be holy. The sacrifice of celibacy meant they gave up the pleasures of marriage and family. We were taught to look upon our priests as "other Christs" and to revere them because they had the power to consecrate and to forgive sins. A celibate "mystique" evolved over time, in which people in the church took on a way of caring for and relating to "Father," bringing him food, gifts, accepting his teaching and his opinions, and looking out for him. Over time, this became deification. Parents would not tolerate any criticism of their priest. Priests generally came to be trusted in virtually any situation and could do no wrong. Nobody, least of all a child, could ever accuse a priest of sexual abuse.

Several factors contribute to a person's decision to become a priest. Certainly the perception of a "calling" manifested in prayer as interest, attraction, and desire to lead a holy life, to do ministry and to lead worship. Training of adolescents in junior seminaries was quite common before the Second Vatican Council. These youths were undergoing training before they arrived at a meaningful psychosexual awareness. In a sense they were psychologically castrated during puberty. (This is akin to the physical castration of choirboys so they could sing in the Sistine Chapel, mentioned later in chapter 15.) Men who entered the seminary after puberty accepted their emasculation at whatever level of sexual maturity they possessed. I say this because personal sexual awareness was to be repressed. Frequently, pedophiles were themselves victimized during their childhood. It is helpful to note that pedophiles are adults who sexually molest prepubescent children while ephebophiles are adults who sexually molest older adolescents.[8] In the sexual abuse crimes of priests in Newfoundland and elsewhere, both kinds of molestations of minors occurred. I believe that priests who sensed but didn't fully understand their sexual tendencies viewed enforced sexual innocence (the celibate mystique) as a safe haven and a means of help to overcome earlier guilt or confusion.

In his book *Papal Sin*, Garry Wills states: "Devout Catholic families will be the least suspicious of a priest's conduct and the most intimidated about challenging the Church. They will also, precisely because of their faith and trust, be the most deeply seared by betrayal."[9] He cites three ways in which a priest pedophile differs from others, all of which are connected with celibacy.

> (1) Because a priest makes a heroic act of self-control, for him to deal with the young is a meeting of the innocent with the innocent, so to speak, and betrayal of God's people is tantamount to being betrayed by God.[10]
>
> (2) Reverence paid to priests because of their heroic act of abstention results in deference, e.g., Catholics are protective and non-Catholics do not wish to offend religious sensibilities.[11]
>
> (3) The most important ingredient with priest pedophilia is that it raises the question whether mandatory celibacy is an unrealizable ideal. When some priests cannot control this most corrupting kind of sexual deviancy, can large numbers of priests control more normal instincts?[12]

We are complex beings and we often act without fully understanding the reasons for our behavior. St. Paul speaks of this inner conflict, "What I do, I do not understand. For I do not do what I want, but I do what I hate" (Rom 7:15). During my police career, I obtained many written statements from offenders confessing to various crimes. I formed the opinion that most crimes are rationalized by their perpetrators to allow them to think that what they are doing "isn't too bad," unless they are totally psychotic. I believe the rationalization of sexual abuse as well as other crimes involves feelings of anger or hatred resulting from the offender's own deprivation or victimization. The Declaration on Religious Liberty (*Dignitatis Humanae*), approved in 1965, teaches that our response to God in faith must be a free response.[13] This new teaching took time to be assimilated and understood. *Compulsory* celibacy is not a free response. The longer they remained in the priesthood and were required to teach and espouse an understanding of religious freedom, the more this reality struck home especially for priests, as described in the Winter Report, "who find celibacy of no value to their priestly ministry" and "for some individuals [for whom it created] excessive and destructive pressures."[14]

A further elaboration of the complexities of the oppressed clerical structure can be seen in two recent books. Eugene Kennedy suggests that clerical spirituality is characterized by a dualistic approach involving warring elements of flesh and spirit, mind and body, intellect and emotions, so that what is healthy is confused with and infected by what is unhealthy and what is holy becomes transgressed or violated. Over the centuries this forced a distorted model of self such that in the living out of that model there was a damaged sense of wholeness and health from which came the sexual wound that cannot be healed until the church first heals its broken notion of the human person.[15]

In the second book, Elizabeth Liebert refers to the dialogue between theology and psychology. She points out that a survey of Roman Catholic spiritual theology between the Council of Trent and Vatican II and the humanistic psychology prevalent in the late 1960s would produce two views of the "ideal person" that are diametrically opposed. The first calls for "death to self" while the second for "self-actualization." She goes on to say that whole classes of persons have been encouraged to internalize submissiveness as a virtue, finding themselves increasingly disenfranchised and impoverished because such submissiveness fosters overdependent relationships and dysfunctional systems that breed addictive and abusive behaviors that tend to be passed on to succeeding generations.[16]

The official hierarchy has not been open to studies about celibate sexuality. When Cardinal John Krol chaired the bishops' committee for multidisciplinary studies of the priesthood in 1969–1971, he argued against research about the sexual behavior of priests.[17] Celibacy's very contentious image became such a sacred topic that nobody, not even the celibates themselves, would discuss it openly. However, the ways that priestly celibacy was lived out were not a secret. Loneliness is one of the results of imposed celibacy. A 1972 study by Father Andrew Greeley in conjunction with the University of Chicago revealed that the desire to marry was the strongest predictor of men planning to leave the priesthood and the primary reason for their wishing to marry was loneliness.[18] Loneliness produces a variety of responses. Some priests have become alcoholics. Some have resorted to homosexual expression. Some are sexually promiscuous and even adulterous. Some have become sexual deviants. Many thousands have retained mistresses. This imposed, permanent, unnatural lifestyle has been destructive for thousands upon thousands of priests. Few if any of these men who failed to live up to the vow of celibacy entered the priesthood intending to default.

Priests became aware that many of their colleagues were leaving active ministry primarily to marry. According to a seminary rector, the exodus of some twenty thousand U.S. priests has given rise to a disproportionate number of priests with a homosexual orientation and created a gay subculture in most of the larger U.S. dioceses. This has ostensibly impacted the self-awareness of many priests if only on a subliminal level of consciousness.[19] Comments from another seminary dean offer a further dimension of the structural system: "The idea that we're special because we're celibate is terribly damaging. That isolationist mentality creates a clerical preserve. It gives people grounds for thinking they're superior. The Roman Curia has no real contact with the real world. That's the deformation."[20]

It can be seen therefore that priest pedophiles and ephebophiles when rationalizing their behavior could well be influenced by their feelings about the exodus of their colleagues to marry or the growing gay subculture, in relation to their own repressed sexuality. Various social changes began to occur in the 1960s. A much greater knowledge of human sexuality came to light from various studies and publicity and a more open attitude toward sexuality was becoming the way of life in the free world.

The Second Vatican Council was a timely corrective to bring the church into the modern world. The ecclesiastical social system began to decentralize and move toward a more collaborative ecclesiastical structure. However, the initial start in implementing the changes began to be reversed in opinion and practice. Those clerics and bishops who opted for change began to be censured. By 1984 Cardinal Ratzinger presented a pessimistic evaluation of the church after the council and introduced the term "restoration." This restoration was ostensibly two-fold, to return to the council's letter and true spirit and to an earlier vision of the faith before the council.[21] Restoration in the sense of "going back," in my experience, is never a viable option.

This unilateral move toward restoration has caused much confusion within the church, because this "high level opinion" was saying that thousands of sincere and dedicated clerics and ecclesial lay ministers in hundreds of dioceses didn't implement the Vatican Council changes well. This gave many people who were not happy with the changes a renewed confidence to challenge the developments that had taken place. In my view this bureaucratic move contravened the Dogmatic Constitution on the Church (*Lumen Gentium*), which decreed that bishops together with Peter's successor are to direct the house of the living God.[22] The absence of authentic consultation with the world's bishops before moving the church backwards is arrogant in the extreme. This arrogant ecclesiastical power has taken over the church since the council. It gained momentum to the point that it limits the authority of bishops within their own jurisdictions and reduces them to the status of puppets in their collegial responsibility for the governance of the universal church. Add to these realities the ingredients of immature or arrested psychosexual development of clerics, loneliness, and the wide berth of acceptance given priests by Catholic families. Here are two descriptions of the problem:

> The crisis in the Catholic Church lies not with the fraction of priests who molest youngsters but in an ecclesiastical power structure that harbors pedophiles, conceals other sexual behavior patterns among its clerics, and uses strategies of duplicity and counterattack against the victims.[23]

> There is a terrible vacuum of leadership at the highest levels of American Catholicism. This vacuum has not just happened. It has been deliberately created by years of episcopal appointments and Vatican interventions designed to prevent the American church from taking national initiatives that might conflict with Rome's. The American bishops' conference has been repeatedly reined in, with power shifted to the cardinals . . . to the point that nothing happens without looking over one's shoulder for approval.[24]

In failing to live up to the promises of Vatican II, the rigid hierarchical Roman Catholic structure evolved into a dysfunctional culture, oppressive of its priests and ultimately of its mission. All in the church have become codependent on this primary stress. For priests who did not leave and who had a tendency to commit crimes of pedophilia or ephebophilia, the dysfunctional and oppressive celibate ecclesiastical structure was ready-made to support their weaknesses. Numerous priests obviously had such tendencies and sexually abused minors. I agree with the laicized priest-psychologist Eugene Kennedy, who stated, "Few if any chose the priesthood in order to have access to or exploit boys and girls."[25] Nevertheless, untold numbers of priests were able to seduce parents into letting them seduce their children within a structure that enabled their deviancy to flourish. This image of the priesthood is grotesque. That is the "systemic" relationship of priest pedophilia and celibacy.

The renewed outcry over clerical sexual abuse of children and cover-ups by the episcopate in the United States received much public comment. A pointed commentary was found on the Internet:

> One consequence of the clergy sex-abuse scandal is that the faulty priorities of the hierarchical system have now been unmasked for the whole world to see, and changes will have to be made. Structures of privilege, secrecy and protection from blame seem to be unraveling before our eyes.
>
> It has been difficult to move from the hierarchical mindset to a more egalitarian model in which all members of the Church enjoy a profound dignity and honor in God's sight. It is even hard for those at the so-called bottom of the pyramid to claim equal dignity for themselves. They have been trained to support the system without question. To some extent, the famous dictum of the late Brazilian educator, Paulo Freire, applies here: *The oppressed internalize the lowly image that the oppressor has of them.*[26]

Along with the sexual abuse of minors but on a much broader scale is a third crisis: **infidelity to the vow of celibacy**. There have been allegations of widespread sexual exploitation of nuns by priests and some bishops in Africa, apparently driven by the clergymen's fear of AIDS. These allegations have been reported in Catholic and secular newspapers throughout the United States. Sister Maura O'Donohue, a member of the Medical Missionaries of Mary and a licensed physician, prepared a formal report of such abuse as early as 1994. Sister O'Donohue reported incidents of abuse in some twenty-three countries on five continents, although the majority occurred in Africa where the AIDS epidemic is most severe and where the subservience of women to men is widely taken for granted by the population at large. There was an indication that among many clergy in Africa the law of celibacy only prohibits marriage.[27]

Particularly significant is the following list of the twenty-three countries where sexual abuse of nuns by Catholic priests has been perpetrated: Botswana, Burundi, Brazil, Colombia, Ghana, India, Ireland, Italy, Kenya, Lesotho, Malawi, Nigeria, Papua New Guinea, Philippines, South Africa, Sierra Leone, Tanzania, Tonga, Uganda, the United States, Zambia, Zaire, and Zimbabwe.[28] I can add that during my seminary experience in 1991 the rector told me that in the minds of some priests celibacy simply means priests cannot marry. However, he unequivocally denounced that point of view. The point I make here is that the existence of this aberration relating to celibacy is known and is another sign of the times that ought not to be overlooked. From the incidents reported in this book and from my personal knowledge, I must add Canada to the above list of countries. In saying this, can there be any doubt that numerous other countries could be added to the list? Just how obvious need this crisis become before the episcopal hierarchy will act? The real question is: How long will it take for the people of God to insist that the choice for celibate living be made optional and thus truly free for those who can observe it?

It is understandable and appropriate that the Catholic faithful as well as other citizens and authorities have taken issue with the sexual abuse of minors by clerics. However, Catholics the world over ought to begin to take issue through the proper channels, with the unnatural law of compulsory celibacy for all clerics. Because the episcopate has been so intent on protecting the image of "priestly innocence," there is little accurate data on which to assess the authenticity of the celibate mandate at large. Yet it seems appropriate in the face of these crises to assess the authenticity of the obligation of celibacy that all candidates for ordination "assumed publicly before God and the Church or professed [by] perpetual vows in a religious institute."[29]

What I understand by the obligation of celibacy is "no sex." Based on a study that suggests two percent of U.S. priests are pedophiles with an additional four percent ostensibly sexually drawn to older youths,[30] and noting that those individuals have a propensity to be sexually active, I would suggest that conservatively four percent of the American priesthood may have sexually abused minors. With a disproportionate number of gay priests, double the number involved in the abuse of minors, or eight percent, may have broken the vow of celibacy by homosexual activity. Double both of those numbers, or twelve percent, may have broken the vow of celibacy by heterosexual activity. This could mean that as many as twenty-five percent of celibate clerics may have failed to live up to the vow of celibacy.

Purporting to assess the authenticity of enforced celibacy illustrates the futility and the anachronism of compulsory celibacy. Is the assessment too low? Too high? Would crimes or broken vows be further categorized as frequent? Infrequent? If these percentages were to translate to hundreds or even thousands of individual priests "at risk," how many hundreds or thousands of "vulnerable" minors, gay men, and heterosexual women might there be? Christians believe in repentance. We believe in a loving, forgiving God. We believe God forgives repentant sinners. The image of the holy celibate priest cast in 1139 was not real. It is defiled. To perpetuate it is a charade, regardless of how many clerics have been faithful. Forced celibacy is not necessary. It is unjust. It is unnatural. It is a crisis of huge proportion.

Should anyone doubt that *power that oppresses* is affecting the church's mission, let us look at a fourth crisis: ***the jeopardizing of sacramental Eucharist***, the sum and summit of Catholic worship. After a recent parish retreat, a visiting priest commented to me that the shortage of priests is beyond crisis proportions. It is now scandalous (if scandal means harming the faith of Christians by our free decisions), because it is saying that celibacy is more important than Eucharist. In my opinion, the people of God are, in effect, being held hostage by a bankrupt and dated sacerdotal adherence to power. This is not the legacy of Jesus Christ. In the matter of Eucharist for the people of God, it is critical to hear what others are saying:

> In a moral theology meant not only for those *under* authority, but equally and especially for those *in* authority, it seems quite clear that Church leaders who create so many specific man-made conditions that hinder a great number of Christian communities and persons from regularly participating in the Eucharist, "commit a grave sin." For should it not be said that Church authorities themselves commit as many sins through their mandates that deprive people of the Eucharist? The point of departure for further deliberation might well be the meal communities of the early Christian Church.[31]

> Most Churchmen now think that Rome abused its authority when, in the Middle Ages or Renaissance, it put whole communities or countries under an interdict (deprivation of all sacraments) in order to punish rulers at odds with the Vatican. But now the Church is imposing a kind of creeping and quiet interdiction when it makes communities do without priests.[32]

> That even great popes draw on inapplicable proof texts from scripture to bolster forgoing sexual relationships is melancholy evidence of how necessary the maintenance of the control of human sexuality

remains for its present organization. So necessary has this discipline become to the Church as an Institution that, in Western countries, the bishops, their collegial spirit lost by their ready cooperation in their own emasculation, are willing to suffer enormous losses in order to keep celibacy in place among the clergy. Such leaders accept their own impotence, for example, in the operational suppression of their national conferences so that they accept—Indeed, make themselves accessories to—the denial of the Eucharist to their Catholic people by refusing to allow married priests or women priests to celebrate this indispensable sacrament of identity and unity. What can it be about the rejection of marriage and the superiority of the so-called higher celibate life that can justify such an extraordinary abandonment of basic pastoral service to their people?[33]

In my work experience outside of the church, I have observed two reactions to people who leave their occupational roles. The first is negative: treating the person leaving as disloyal, a quitter, not able to cope, letting down the company or the organization. The person leaving when this negative attitude prevails is actually shunned or made to feel shunned. The other reaction I have witnessed is positive. The person leaving hears expressions of disappointment over the loss of their contribution toward the goals of the company or organization but at the same time receives inquiries as to their future well-being with extended good wishes and encouragement. This more positive attitude presupposes the integrity of the personal decision, applauds the hope expressed for personal betterment, and encourages the person. The more positive, expectant, loving response speaks volumes about the disposition, nature of dedication, and exercise of authority of those who were in relationship with the person who made the decision to leave. This latter response is "more Christian," but unfortunately it has not been the general practice in the Catholic Church. This leads us to a fifth crisis: ***the failure to forgive priests for leaving active ministry***.

Monsignor William H. Shannon, a priest for fifty-five years, expressed sorrow over priests leaving active ministry. Shannon's sorrow is not about the decision those priests have made but over the way they have been treated. He cites the laicization process that deprives these men of their priestly faculties but also deprives them of ministries that rightfully belong to all the baptized. As an example, former priests are forbidden to teach in Catholic institutions despite their qualifications, are not allowed to participate in catechetical programs in a parish community, and cannot serve as lectors, servers, or eucharistic ministers. They become less than laypersons. In effect, they are treated as nonpersons in the church community. A special sorrow of the author is that we, the church, are not allowed to celebrate the years of service these men gave to the church. He suggests they left quietly, often painfully. He hopes for the day when those men who wish to do so will once again be allowed to exercise priestly ministry, and calls for their immediate restoration to the full status of baptized members of the Body of Christ.[34]

When a priest wishes to leave active ministry honorably, the process is referred to as laicization, that is, returning to the lay state. When a priest "loses the clerical state," to use the wording of canon 290 §1, it is "by a judicial decision or administrative decree which declares the invalidity of sacred ordination." The outgoing priest is required to accept the decision or decree that his ordination was invalid at its outset. How humiliating and oppressive! Commentary suggests that these canons were put in place because data from petitioners in the laicization processes alleged insufficient freedom and understanding at the time of their ordination.[35] However well intentioned, the attempt at "enforcing the enforcement" of innocence was likewise doomed to failure.

These men were initially required by canon 1036 to put in writing that they were freely choosing to be ordained, and by canon 1037 to publicly assume the obligation of celibacy. Moreover, canon 291 insists that this loss of the clerical state does not dispense from the obligation of celibacy, which is reserved to the Roman Pontiff alone. This is manipulative control of the worst kind. It has been likened to a decree of nullity in marriage cases. However, I submit it is not the same as a decree of nullity in marriage. I served for eight years as an advocate for petitioners seeking marriage annulments from church tribunals. I believe a finding of invalidity at the time of the exchange of marriage vows is possible, because marriage is a covenant between two persons before God that is to be *mutually given and received*. Evidence revealing a disparity of intent, such as error, grave lack of discretion, etc., could substantiate and thus "invalidate" marriage as understood in the Christian context. Such a finding does not deny the relationship nor render any children illegitimate. The process attempts to segregate the spiritual and the civil in very meaningful if not highly charged emotional circumstances. The sacrament of orders, on the other hand, is between the candidate and God. Only God ought to grant a judicial decision of "invalidity" and an administrative decree should not have to allege "invalidity."

For many people, the marriage annulment process is difficult and for some it is oppressive. Despite this, there is strength in what can be a cathartic process for parties willing to invest themselves to derive greater self-knowledge for their future well-being, especially when they plan to remarry. Competent advice and advocacy are essential to achieving these benefits. Tribunal procedures are only instituted after a marriage has been subject to a civil decree of divorce, lest the church be accused of counseling bigamy. Moreover, in sacramental marriage there can be no "conditions" agreed upon beforehand, when these would invalidate the free and mutual gift of self in the exchange of vows. Yet a candidate for orders is obliged to agree to the condition of living a celibate life. I believe this imposition upon every candidate vitiates the vow of orders because it is an unjust condition.

In matters of ecclesiastical jurisprudence, we already have a terrible memory of the church's inquisitorial practices in the Middle Ages. In my tribunal advocacy responsibilities, I was frequently reminded and indeed wondered at times if, in fact, I too was perpetuating the insidious *power that oppresses*. Holding in the midst of the legalese that my intent was to facilitate healing and growth of people wounded by their failed marriage, I nonetheless recognize what a fine line there is when we attempt to play God by rendering judgment on people or their conduct.

The principal crisis in the priesthood, I believe, arose from the unnatural law urged upon married clerics for seven hundred years and then vindictively imposed for the next eight hundred years on all priests, because babies were still being born to the former married clerics. History reveals a secondary motive for this unnatural law was to ensure that the church rather than a priest's family would inherit a priest's estate. That motive without some qualification or just distribution can also be seen as oppressive. Whatever the motives were that aimed at suppressing human sexuality for clerics, the effects have been devastating. The mission of Jesus has been seconded to the arrogance of ecclesiastical power.

Centuries of forced sexual renunciation produced priests castrated in their power to create and re-create. Their power to transform the world is limited to building the institution. They cannot speak out even when they disagree. Their educational process integrated them into an ecclesiastical system designed to bring about conformity to the system. The 1965 Declaration on Religious Liberty meanwhile became the means by which thousands of priests began to deal critically and creatively with reality and the transformation of their world. Why else did one hundred thousand priests leave? It also became the means, albeit more slowly, by which the baptized believers began to deal creatively with reality and with their transformation.

This analysis of the ordained priesthood in crises would not be complete if it did not identify a missing element that is also, ultimately a consequence of *power that oppresses.* This missing element is actually a void—a void so significant that it diminishes the integrity of the ordained priesthood in a church that claims to hold that "there exists among all the Christian faithful a true equality with regard to dignity" (canon 208) and that "the Christian faithful have the right to receive assistance from the sacred pastors out of the spiritual goods of the Church, especially the word of God and the sacraments" (canon 213). I am speaking about **the absence of ordained women.** My understanding of dignity, which I have taught in the church for several years, is self-respect, self-worth, and value as a person. I believe that if we as a people have this dignity at all, we have it because we are loved unconditionally by the God who created us.

A commentary on canon law informs us that the Second Vatican Council listed word and sacrament as constitutive elements of the church's mission. The right to receive them is rooted in baptism and is not a privilege granted by church authorities, but is a claim rooted in the action of Christ that empowers Christians to seek the services of their pastors. It is the first of several rights mentioned for laypersons and all Christians in the Dogmatic Constitution on the Church (*Lumen Gentium,* 37)[36] Unfortunately, because of the existing tradition when the Code of Canon Law was revised in 1983, it was found necessary to re-enact canon 1024, which states, "Only a baptized male validly receives sacred ordination." The commentary reveals that the literature on this canon during the revision process exceeded the total amount of literature on all the other canons relating to orders.[37]

In my quest to be ordained as a married man I became aware that I am "simply impeded from receiving orders" as "a man who has a wife, unless [I am] legitimately destined for the permanent diaconate" (canon 1042 §1). Commentary in relation to this canon points out that marriage is an impediment to canon 277 §1, which states:

> Clerics are obliged to observe perfect and perpetual continence for the sake of the kingdom of heaven and therefore are obliged to observe celibacy, which is a special gift of God, by which sacred ministers can adhere more easily to Christ with an undivided heart and

can more freely dedicate themselves to the service of God and humankind.[38]

I believe that canon 277 is in error because it imposes celibacy as a special gift of God across the board on every person who perceives a call to the ordained ministry. It may be a special gift of God for some people but our knowledge and experience as human beings unequivocally confirms marriage as the natural order for most people. Celibacy is thus an *unnatural (canon) law*. Having pointed to two significant voids impinging on the "the ordained priesthood in crises" in addition to five major crises, I am dismayed because *power that oppresses* has inhibited the collegial efforts of the world's bishops intended as the "Light of Nations" (*Lumen Gentium*) and has dimmed the light of Christ in the world.

In the Catholic tradition, expressing the opinion that canon law is in error is serious. But even mentioning the absence of ordained women is unthinkable, because it questions the apostolic letter of Pope John Paul II to all bishops entitled *Ordinatio Sacerdotalis* (1994). Specifically the letter states: "I declare that the church has no authority whatsoever to confer priestly ordination on women and that this judgment is to be definitively held by all the Church's faithful." I am a believing Catholic Christian. There is no protocol for me to question the awesome authority of the successor of St. Peter. The only legitimate claim I may cling to is the "obedience of faith" spoken of by St. Paul (Rom 1:5 and 16:26) cited in the Catholic Catechism at 2087 and further clarified by 2217: "Children should also obey the reasonable directions of their teachers and all to whom their parents have entrusted them. But if a child is convinced in conscience that it would be morally wrong to obey a particular order, he must not do so."[39] If I cannot definitively hold the judgment that the church has no authority to confer priestly ordination on women, what do the world's bishops really believe about this? Are they bound by feudal rule or an oath that restricts their freedom?

I do know that a book written by a nun in support of the ordination of women has been suppressed at the episcopal level of my church. I was told this when I called the office of the Liturgical Press in Collegeville, Minnesota, which published this book in the United States after it was first published in the United Kingdom in 1994 but which now dutifully declares the book "out of print." I imagine it would be painful for the episcopate to read that when women are told they may not represent Christ, that is, that they may not stand *in persona Christi*, they feel disowned and disempowered at their most profound level—the level of their very being.[40] I reject the restoration of medieval censorship and any attempt to ascribe a retroactive infallibility to this apostolic letter. In conscience I must reject this as *power that oppresses,* because it lacks the collegial community of discernment so essential for the life of the church.

Having alleged power that oppresses as the underlying cause of these several crises in the priesthood, I am impelled to offer some insight toward a resolution. To do this I, too, refer to the noted Brazilian educator of liberation Paulo Freire. He wrote that a concern for humanization leads us to recognize dehumanization. Dehumanization is the result of an unjust order that engenders violence in the oppressors, which in turn dehumanizes the oppressed. Of the two realities, humanization is our true vocation. The central problem he cites is this: How can the oppressed, as divided, unauthentic beings, participate in developing the pedagogy of their liberation? Only as they discover themselves to be "hosts" of the oppressor can they contribute to the midwifery of their liberating pedagogy. As long as they live in the duality in which to be is to be like, and to be like is to be like the oppressor, this contribution is impossible. The pedagogy of the oppressed is an instrument for their critical discovery that both they and their oppressors are manifestations of dehumanization. However, the oppressed in seeking to regain their humanity are called to become not oppressors of the oppressors but restorers of the humanity of both. I believe that the great humanistic and historical task of the oppressed in the church is for the oppressed to liberate themselves and their oppressors as well. Freire's theory for this resolution is that the oppressors who exploit and control by virtue of their power cannot find the strength in their power to liberate either the oppressed or themselves. The reason is that the oppressor who is himself dehumanized because he dehumanizes others is unable to lead this struggle. Only the power that springs from the weakness of the oppressed will be sufficiently strong to free both.[41]

The church's legacy from the sixteenth-century Counter Reformation emphasized uniformity at the expense of unity. It created seminaries where men went in different but came out the same. With the rise of lay ecclesial ministers, in the absence of specific training, the focus was to "be like" the ordained. With the increased involvement of lay ministers, criticisms have been made of the clericalist attitudes of lay ministers. This emphasis and focus on "sameness" promotes mediocrity. The five crises that I have described are actually symptoms of *power that oppresses.*

People who believe they are called to ministry are predisposed to giving themselves in service to others. It is very easy for them to internalize submissiveness as a virtue, as Elizabeth Liebert has described, and to fall into a disenfranchised and impoverished system wherein they actually "host" oppressive control. This is the time in the history of the church when its members need to work together to overcome the oppression that its episcopal administrators are unable to overcome. The power that springs from our oppression will be the strength that moves ecclesial leadership from the *power that oppresses* to an *authority that liberates.*

11

MY CALL TO PRIESTHOOD

> For who has stood in the Council of the Lord so as to see and hear his word? Who has given heed to his word so as to proclaim it?
>
> Jeremiah 23:18

It is quite remarkable how we learn and grow. Throughout my married life I was involved and interested in ministry, whereas Irene, though compassionate, was a more private person. I would regularly visit the hospital or otherwise be involved in some church or community activity. While Irene was always interested and happy to hear about these things, she was more content to be at home with the affairs of the children and to support and encourage me in those activities outside the home. It had been a mutual decision that Irene would not work outside of the home, and the years of my responding to police calls after hours in rural settings had largely set the pattern for Irene to prefer to remain at home.

In retrospect, I need to take responsibility for the patriarchal bent that we both bought into at the outset of our marriage. I say this because Irene became a Catholic and together we adopted the prevailing patriarchal view, believing it to be a principal value for our lives. I write this because I believe Irene was coming to the realization that her acceptance of the subordinate role was in fact a denial of her equality of dignity. Irene was not yet able to articulate her impression, but I think she was coming to that awareness before it began to dawn on me. Having survived her in life, I have come to reject the patriarchal stance in favor of a more "mutual" relatedness in marriage.

Irene died on January 30, 1987. Our daughter Monica had traveled from Edmonton to be with her that afternoon. When I was home for lunch, Irene began asking for more pain medication. It had been more than twenty-four hours since her last injection. I conferred with Irene to try to ascertain if the pain had truly recurred or if her request was made as a form of insurance. Irene made it clear it was for pain. Monica then administered the pain medication and I said goodbye and went to work.

It was about 5:30 P.M. when Monica called me. She was crying and was unable to rouse Irene and was feeling upset because she herself had dozed off. I told her not to be concerned, that we anticipated this would occur at some time and assured her I would be right home. I arrived within about ten minutes and I noticed that Irene was barely breathing. I called 911 and the paramedics arrived. I asked if they could block the pain medication Irene had received earlier, and they indicated they could but were reluctant to do so. Irene had very little pulse yet it seemed to me that perhaps we could assist her breathing. The paramedics agreed and they hooked Irene up to an oxygen tank. Irene seemed to benefit and her pulse became stronger. I requested they take Irene to the hospital, thinking that if anything else could be done a physician and necessary equipment would be available.

Monica drove to the hospital and I went in the ambulance with Irene. On the way to the hospital, I asked Irene if she was all right and her last words were "I'm all right, I'm all right!" We went to the emergency admitting area and a nurse was with us intermittently. Monica and I remained with Irene, and when the nurse indicated it would be a matter of time, I left to call Father Duncan to attend. He was tied up in a liturgy at the time but called for a priest to come from St. Mary's Parish. This priest arrived and joined Monica and me and Irene. Since her last words to me in the ambulance, Irene was no longer able to communicate but was breathing and lying on a gurney in the Red Deer Hospital emergency room. The priest began reading from scripture and as he pronounced the words "Jesus returned to Capernaum," Irene turned her head toward the priest and her eyes became teary. I blurted out to the priest "she knows you're here," inadvertently interrupting him in his reading of the gospel. The priest then anointed Irene's forehead and hands, bade us farewell, and left.

Within about ten minutes Irene stopped breathing. I watched as her carotid artery slowly stopped beating. I remained holding her hand and I wanted to stay until Irene's hand would become cold, but the nurse and Monica encouraged me to leave. Monica and I drove back to the house and then I drove to the restaurant where John was working. I asked someone to have John come to see me in a room where we could be alone. I was ushered to a small upstairs room. John came in and I told him that his mother had died. Together we cried for several minutes, until we decided he would go back to work, and I left.

The next couple of days were very busy. I asked Duncan if he would hold the funeral on Monday because it was February 2, the feast of the Presentation and the day when Monica, Veronica, and John had all been baptized. It was Duncan's usual day off and he agreed provided I could make the arrangements with the cemetery. I was able to do this through the city clerk whom I knew from work, and he arranged to have the grave opened at an additional cost due to having to thaw the frozen ground. Arrangements were made and many of our friends and immediate family attended, together with Father Lucien Morrissette from Athabasca who was present with Duncan in the sanctuary. With the help of the choir, I was able to lead the singing and I also gave the reflection. The choir was very helpful and supportive as was Duncan. Our children and their spouses and many friends attended.

In the days and weeks following the funeral, I was emotionally lost. John lived with me so that I had company and I appreciated that. I continued to work but I began to wonder why I needed a big house and a fancy car. One day a Pentecostal minister, who came to see me about the purchase of land, talked with me about the loss of Irene. His parting words were "Stay close to God." I continued to stay close to God and the church. In April I took a "grief and loss recovery seminar" at the suggestion of my eldest son, Eugene.

In June I took a trip to Minneapolis to attend the National Pastoral Musicians Conference. I met people there who related with me in my grief in spiritual ways, which was comforting. The music experience was wonderful. In August I attended a weeklong seminar in Calgary to learn about the Rite of Christian Initiation of Adults, which is the way inquirers learn about the Catholic faith. It was during these excursions in the faith that I felt moved to explore the possibility of becoming a priest. Friends and acquaintances who encouraged me in that direction buoyed up this desire. I thought about this a great deal. The shortage of priests made this seem more urgent. I was fifty-one years of age and I considered that I could become eligible for ordination by the time I was fifty-seven and could serve for fifteen or more years. I had no interest in establishing a relationship with another woman.

I spoke to Duncan about this and he gave me a brochure and suggested I write to the second career seminary that had been established in Spokane, Washington. I did this and was contacted by Father Armand Nigro, S.J., rector of that seminary. Duncan suggested I write to Archbishop MacNeil in Edmonton, which I did. I met with him on a couple of occasions. On one of my visits with Archbishop MacNeil, my daughter Monica had just given birth to her second daughter, Jesse, at the General Hospital in Edmonton, not far from the Chancery Office. It was October 14, 1987. I visited Monica before seeing the archbishop. While I was with the archbishop, he suggested I take the view from John's Gospel to "come and see." He felt that, were I to go to the seminary and find the studies too much or otherwise find that the calling was not for me, I would at least have given it a valiant try. When I left the archbishop and went to St. Joseph's Cathedral to pray, I noticed a Bible in the pew. I picked it up and it opened at one of the Hebrew Scripture readings that talked of war upon war, which caused me immediately to turn to the New Testament. Remarkably, it opened at the page that held the quote "come and see"! This was at the very least coincidental, but from a faith perspective it was an affirmation of hope.

I arranged to spend a few days at St. Joseph's Seminary in Edmonton. I was given a room and attended a number of classes as well as mass with the seminarians. I had been to that seminary on many occasions, having served on the Knights of Columbus Vocations Team in the late 1970s. On one occasion during mass, when all were called to stand around the altar, I found myself feeling very much at home, and during the consecration becoming very emotional and unable to stop tears from flowing. After the death of Irene, I had shed many tears, but these were different. These tears were accompanied by awe in the realization that I felt drawn to the priesthood and at the same time I was afraid. It was like the two emotions—desire and fear of the unknown—were one. In the midst of my tears it was scary! I think it was my coming to the full awareness that I was preparing to leave my children and their families and the achievements of my second career, but with an underlying calm assurance that I needed to do this. I thoroughly enjoyed the classes, speaking with the men, and generally feeling that I could be comfortable in that environment.

I later made arrangements to stay at Mater Dei Institute of Priestly Formation in Spokane, and Father Duncan accompanied me on the trip. We drove in my car and shared the driving. I was grateful for his companionship. It was especially meaningful for me, since Duncan had accompanied Irene and me through the latter part of her illness. The seminary building in Spokane was not as large and well built as in Edmonton, and some of the men, particularly one or two of the deacons, seemed unnecessarily authoritarian. Gonzaga University, on the other hand, was a wonderful campus, more than a hundred years old. It was November. The leaves had not yet fallen and the grounds and trees were very beautiful. Because of Mater Dei's affiliation with Gonzaga University, I would be able to obtain formal degree accreditation, whereas the Edmonton seminary could not offer that. The seminarians in Spokane consisted of twenty-six men whose average age corresponded to my fifty-two years. A similar number of seminarians in Edmonton were younger, having an average age of thirty-eight years. Another consideration for me was the thought that I ought to be detached from friends and family for greater application to studies. I remember one evening after dark, standing on the front steps of Mater Dei Institute, looking at the streetscape and just "knowing" that I would be living there. A little of the earlier feeling of awe experienced during the consecration at St. Joseph's Seminary presented itself again, along with some of the emotion. After visiting both seminaries, my preference was for Spokane.

Prior to gaining admission to Mater Dei Institute, I was required to document what I perceived were the signs of God's call for me to pursue the ordained ministry. I sketched the development of my awareness of a call from God beginning with my training as an altar boy in St. Boniface Cathedral in Manitoba when I was eight years old. I included the times at nine years of age when my older brother and I used to pretend "saying mass." I was ten years old when our family moved to Kamloops, where I continued altar serving until I was seventeen. About three months after the death of Irene the inclination became stronger. I had told Irene when we planned to marry that if anything happened to her I would never remarry. My mother's example in remaining a widow for thirty years after the passing of my father seemed to me to be an inspiration. I had asked for prayers of three couples and from three or four other individuals with whom I had shared my inclination. My own prayer life had intensified with a view to discerning the authenticity of this calling and I considered that I was as certain of the call as I had been of my earlier decision to marry. Additional information was requested of me in the completion of the Mater Dei application documents. This included all manner of personal history, academics, health, social history, financial situation, Catholic practice, references, relationships, occupations, and spirituality. In addition I was asked to describe an ideal priest in today's church. Quoting from my original application, this is what I identified at that time:

- Organized in prayer, office administration, and use of time.
- Has superior management skills in matters of coordination and delegation so as to draw the best out of the greatest possible numbers of people in building community.
- Able to communicate well in homilies as well as personally with staff, parishioners, chancery office, and the bishop.
- Works to specific objectives which have been developed with and for the parish community.
- Adept at following personal objectives which he has developed over time and which integrate well with the parish objectives.
- Able to bring to bear various forms of expertise to assist in the growth and development of the parish community.

I record the idealism in this writing, because it is part of this presentation of a "sign of the times" and will be expanded upon in succeeding chapters. During my visit in Spokane, I related to Armand Nigro what the archbishop had told me concerning the words "come and see," and that if it didn't work out I would have given it a valiant try. Armand countered: "No disrespect to your archbishop, but don't come here if you are just trying to find out if you have a vocation. You better know, because otherwise it never works!"

One of the requirements for entry to Mater Dei was to make a one-week directed retreat, which I did at the Providence Center in Edmonton shortly before leaving for Spokane. This was my first personally directed retreat, which I enjoyed very much. My reason for attending the retreat and my aspirations toward a "late vocation" as a priest were at the heart of my assignments. Each day the retreat director would meet with me and propose an assignment for reflection and prayer.

On the last day of my retreat, my assignment was to "ask for the job"! In a spiritual sense, all of us pray to God, either directly or with the help of others, hoping to receive "an answer." On that day I began praying in the main chapel but found this wanting because of its size and the occasional distraction. So I moved to a smaller upstairs chapel where the Eucharist was also kept. My prayer that day was both directly to Christ whom I believed to be truly present in the Blessed Sacrament and through Mary, his mother. I had never spent this much time in such a concerted prayer effort. I have since mused that perhaps I felt I could get through to God better in smaller quarters. Was there "an answer" for me that day? Yes, definitely. I came away from those hours of reflection and petition with two "answers." I came to these in the depth of my being, without any words being heard but nonetheless as two distinct feelings or dispositions concerning my aspiration. The first, which I sensed came from the mother of Christ, was that of "encouragement." The second, which I sensed to have been from Jesus, was "You're on the right track, but you haven't got the job yet."

I didn't know what that all meant, except that it served to move me closer to entering the seminary than to abandoning the idea—even with Armand Nigro's admonition: "Don't come here if you are just trying to find out if you have a vocation. You better know!" My instincts confirmed that at least I was on the right track. I felt I could cope with the mandatory requirement of celibacy, thinking that my children and their families would help to sustain me should I become lonely. I did not wish to re-marry, because I did not wish to go through a major illness again, which might be expected either in my case or that of a new spouse. Neither did I wish to embrace the added responsibilities of an extended family in the event of remarriage.

When all the essential information was received and it appeared that I would be accepted in the seminary and at Gonzaga University, I resigned from my position as regional manager after nine years with Melcor Developments Ltd. My sons and sons-in-law had divided up my household furnishings and equipment in advance of "moving day," when they came with a large rented truck and loaded up the contents of my house, except for the personal items that I would retain. I rented my house because market conditions precluded an immediate sale. My eldest son, Eugene, agreed to assist me in my move to Spokane. My limited furniture and personal effects were loaded onto Eugene's pick-up truck. He and his wife, Donna, led the way to Spokane, and I followed in an older car which had been Irene's parents' vehicle, and which I retrieved from my son John. We booked into a motel that evening. The next day we went to the seminary. They helped me unload my effects into my assigned room to which Father Nigro escorted us, left my car and me, and departed in their pick-up. I was there! A third-career seminarian at fifty-two years of age and by the grace of God a priest for fifteen (plus or minus) years! This would be my contribution toward alleviating the priest shortage.

And where else than Mater Dei—the Mother of God Institute? It was May 1988.

The seminary was a two-story former convent, about three blocks from Gonzaga University. On the main floor were a chapel, offices, library, large parlor, kitchen and dining area, and a guestroom. My room was at the top of the stairs from the main entrance to the seminary. The room itself was nine by twelve. I had brought my own bed, bookcase, and desk. There was a built-in closet and sink in the room. The bathroom and showers were down the hall. The view from my window was gorgeous, looking onto the lawn and a small grotto to Mary, with a backdrop of very tall mature pine trees surrounding the housetops from the level of my second-story window.

My studies began that summer. All went well, considering that I had not been in school for thirty-five years. I enjoyed studying. I am grateful to Father Nigro, and to Monsignor John Zeder, who became rector about the time of my arrival. In a very special way I am grateful to Father Charles Skok, who accepted me for spiritual direction and continued in that capacity to my benefit during my entire stay in Spokane. Meals were mostly taken in the university cafeteria, supplemented by the seminary kitchen where we could provide our own food and do our own cooking or snacking. By the time I arrived, a number of seminarians had returned to their dioceses, and not all of the men stayed for summer classes.

An event that had been planned before I arrived at the Spokane seminary but was to take place in Calgary on June 5 was the fiftieth anniversary of the ordination of Eugene Violini. I had been part of the planning for the celebration that was to take place in the rear yard of Eugene's house. I had arranged for a friend from the music ministry in Red Deer to travel to Calgary with two instrumentalists and his portable electric piano, so that there would be accompaniment while I led the singing. I flew back for this event, which was well attended by many people who knew Eugene over the years. I kept in touch with Eugene during my seminary days, and whenever I was in Calgary I would attend mass in the chapel of his home. He had been in poor health for years and had suffered much. He continued in his priestly ministry in retirement, and many people used to come to him for the sacrament of penance. Once or twice I raised the issue of his "unofficial" parish within the cathedral parish jurisdiction, which he staunchly defended! It was more out of friendly joshing that I dared challenge his "retirement" ministry, because Eugene always followed the guidelines of the bishop and the magisterium to perfection.

My first summer at the seminary I met a student by the name of Julius Onyango-Akidi, a member of the Marian Brothers from the diocese of Arua, Uganda. He lived in one of the additional houses reserved for seminarians and men striving to become seminarians. He was performing janitorial tasks to satisfy part of the costs of his education and lodging. We shared a great deal as colleagues in learning. I hosted him in some travel to Canada and in the United States, taking him to meet my family and friends in Alberta and to Disneyland in California. Brother Julius had very little resources and his order was quite impoverished, having suffered from the ravages of two dictators and the accompanying civil unrest.

There were two sabbatical programs offered each year by the university for priests and vowed religious men and women. The seminarians came to know those on sabbatical and socialized with them at mealtimes, on occasional gatherings, and in some classes. In the fall semester of 1988, I met a woman religious who had been a missionary in Africa. She was a member of a religious order from Ireland and had experienced "burn out" after an eight-year assignment in Africa. I shall call her Mary. I was quite taken by the fact that she was the same age as Irene, yet her entire life had been spent as a nun, working to build up the body of Christ in a foreign land. Irene on the other hand had spent twenty-seven years in sacramental marriage with me and had given birth to five children. Mary was quite tired and still recovering from her ordeal, and this social contact was mutually insightful and helpful.

At Christmastime, I returned to Canada to visit my family. The visit was good. I returned in January, anxious to get back to my new routine. I found myself looking for Mary in the few days before classes resumed. This concerned me somewhat, and I discussed this attraction with another woman religious who was an experienced clinical psychologist, also on sabbatical from Canada. Her thoughts were that I ought not to be concerned as this was quite natural and the mutual sharing would be therapeutic. Indeed, this turned out to be the case, for when the spring semester ended, Mary remained for a thirty-day retreat and then left for Ireland. We corresponded at intervals for more than a year. Mary returned to her missionary role in Africa, and I have since lost contact with her.

My first three years and three summers were spent completing my undergraduate education, but consisted of religious subjects once the required courses were completed. I returned to Canada for a couple of weeks each summer and each Christmas, spending time with one or more of my children and grandchildren. One Christmas, I drove a seminarian who was studying for that diocese to St. Paul, Alberta. Some twenty years earlier I had been in charge of the RCMP Detachment in Bonnyville, thirty miles northeast of St. Paul. My seminarian colleague and I had experienced a let-down when exams were over, after four months of rigorous study. We left Spokane right after exams and were quite tired. The bishop of St. Paul was very hospitable and recommended that I stay a couple of days to rest up. I accepted, and while there I took a leisurely drive to Bonnyville where I renewed old acquaintances. I visited with some native Métis people whom I had known previously and with the parish priest at Bonnyville whom I had known prior to my marriage when I was stationed at Mayerthorpe. The visit was very meaningful for me. It offered sufficient respite for me before visiting with my daughters and my grandchildren in Edmonton.

Each successive break from studies meant a visit with family and then a return to the seminary for a short retreat, before starting the next semester. I shall always treasure those days spent in learning, meeting new people, and experiencing new growth and understanding in my faith. My traditional sense of theology changed markedly during those three years. I was impressed by the insights of modern scripture study and especially by the fact that the church had seemingly kept pace with change and growth in society. However, my experience in the church since my seminary days have revealed just how slowly the church does change.

During my fourth summer at the seminary, with the encouragement of Archbishop MacNeil, I attended a three-month training unit of Clinical Pastoral Education (CPE) at Deaconess Hospital in Spokane. In my life prior to entering the seminary, I had achieved what I considered to be a reasonable degree of self-actualization, largely with the help of Irene. I think now that what I had achieved in my earlier careers was a certain knowledge and training, and the discipline to apply that knowledge which enabled me to adapt to my career change and to mellow somewhat in my family relationships.

CPE was an in-depth practicum in conjunction with my graduate studies at Gonzaga University. Four mornings a week were spent in psychotherapeutic analysis. Our group was supervised by a Methodist minister and consisted of two women Episcopal seminarians, two Catholic seminarians, and a Catholic nun who unfortunately left the group early due to illness in her family. In one of our many discussions, a gender issue came up and I remember expressing doubt about the capacity of women to be in ministry. Naturally, I was challenged to clarify what I was saying. All I could answer at the time was that the only ministry I had ever experienced was that of a male priest.

It wasn't long after I began working side by side with women in hospital ministry that I realized that "being Christ" for someone has nothing to do with gender. A woman can be Christ for me just as well as a man, and indeed in certain situations her relatedness could be more Christ-like than that of a man. What began to happen once I got past the question of gender was to assess my own capacity to be in ministry. The saving feature about my ignorance is that I was later able to share with the group a moving experience with a family in a grief situation, and I was able to express my relief that, yes, I believed I could do ministry. For their part, my colleagues rejoiced with me in my growing and learning. Looking back on that today, I can hardly believe I was that ignorant about ministry, but more importantly it revealed to me how much we are conditioned by past practices and by entrenched and oppressive social systems, even those of church traditions.

To illustrate just how entrenched social practices are, I was first introduced to a raised consciousness regarding the role of women by Sister Bernadette O'Neil, who, as I've mentioned, served as a pastoral assistant at Sacred Heart Parish in Red Deer. On more than one occasion I confronted her and accused her of being a feminist with a chip on her shoulder. More than once Bernie, as we called her, gave me some articles to read. I considered myself quite up to date in this matter of the role of women. In fact, I had given a talk to a group of Catholic women in Red Deer on this raised consciousness. While I succeeded in helping some of those women to come to a deeper awareness of their role, I myself was only partially enlightened to understanding the true equality of dignity of women.

My ignorance about women in ministry clearly had been so deeply entrenched that I now recognize it was a bias and a form of discriminating against women that I had aquired early and perpetuated most of my adult life. I have frequently thought of Bernie and her efforts to help me recognize what she understood because of the oppression that she experienced as a woman in the church. Naturally, there is a theological understanding concerning this equality of dignity that I now hold, thanks to the fact that women theologians have been able to articulate and express this truth. This theological understanding is fundamental to understanding the historical oppression of women in the Catholic Church and how that oppression actually transferred to me.

The formation for hospital ministry required reading, the writing of papers, personal goal setting, and the submission of written verbatims based on actual but anonymously presented facts for group evaluation. Members of the group took turns being the chaplain on call overnight, and thus many hours were devoted to this training. Relaxation consisted of walks and discussion with colleagues who were pursuing this ministry. The group met occasionally with a larger group of "permanent" resident chaplains in training to complete four units of three months each, generally required for professional employment as full-time hospital chaplains.

One of the resident chaplain trainees consistently worked in the intensive care unit (ICU) and attended the morning update meetings to learn whatever may have transpired during the night that would require follow-up by the day chaplains. Her name was Jan, a Catholic woman who was completing her residency that quarter. I was attracted to her initially by her residency photo circulated in the various hospital departments. Jan was away on vacation when our group started. From her picture I had the impression that I had seen her or met her before, yet neither her name nor her background were known to me. Something about her picture intrigued me. I first met Jan at a meeting of the combined CPE resident and summer groups after she had returned from vacation. Jan was a little different than her picture, but very pretty and petite. She wore makeup, nice earrings, and was always well dressed.

It was now four years after Irene's untimely passing, and I was in the latter part of the CPE program. Jan and I served together on two or three occasions in the ICU where we experienced a unique compatibility in collaborative ministry. I was attracted to Jan who was preparing for professional ministry. She possessed similar characteristics to Irene, both in age and appearance.

Up until that time, I had met several women religious from various ministries in the United States and from a number of other countries. I was in fact very committed to pursuing what was in effect my "third career," believing that I would have the best of both worlds as a celibate priest, widower, father, and grandfather. However, prior to the CPE training, I had two other relationships with women religious during my four years at Mater Dei, that were born essentially out of my need for companionship. These stand out like the circumstances of my becoming acquainted with Mary, the missionary nun from Africa, but involved a greater degree of personal sharing and recreation.

These relationships were "safe" encounters with committed religious women, but in retrospect they served to set the stage for me to meet Jan. My attraction to Jan grew in the course of extensive hours of work. Over the summer we spent some time walking and sharing. At times we assisted one another with ministry. This relationship developed to the point that I fell in love with Jan. The realization that I could spend the rest of my life with her simply evolved and the question loomed "now what do I do?" Should I go back to the seminary in September and continue studies that I knew were leading me to embrace a celibate lifestyle? Was I being true to myself? What of the expectations of the archbishop? My children? I began to experience considerable anxiety.

Before entering the seminary, I had asked Ralph Young, my supervisor at Melcor, to complete a recommendation form for my acceptance at Mater Dei Institute. He did so, but at one point before I left Melcor Ralph mentioned to me that there was one question for which he didn't know the answer, and that was his opinion of my suitability to be celibate. In the course of discernment, one needs to be open to the love of God manifested in many areas and aspects of life. Why I didn't put more stock in Ralph's observation relating to celibacy I am not sure. I can't recall the exact timing of his sharing with me, except that it was toward the time of my final acceptance at Mater Dei. I think there were other factors militating against my ability to hear whether I was a suitable candidate for celibacy or not. Certainly I had thought about it, but in the immediate years following her demise, I could not visualize another woman replacing Irene.

During my earlier work experience, I became a student of decision-making processes, particularly for times when decision-making information is either limited or unavailable. Usually this was in matters of investigative strategies anticipating probable outcomes and the gathering of evidence, or of critical business decisions forecasting market risk factors a year or more in advance. In such circumstances, when all the relevant information is not at hand but a need to act is imminent, one goes on "gut feelings" based upon one's total insight, knowledge, and experience.

When we endeavor to discern the will of God for ourselves, I submit that we operate in much the same way as conventional or secular decision-making processes. The major difference is that of faith, which requires prayer and listening. Implicit with the gift of faith is the dictum of St. Augustine, "To know yourself is to know God." Stated another way by Julian of Norwich in the fourteenth century: "We will never fully know God until we come to know ourselves thoroughly."

Perhaps it was my retreat that kept me persevering in my goal to attend the seminary and made me unable to hear Ralph Young. Although I thought that I had a good knowledge of self when I decided to enter the seminary, my self-knowledge is much deeper now. For the longest time I didn't know what Augustine meant when he said "To know yourself is to know God." What helped me the most in coming closer to knowledge of myself was the CPE practicum that the archbishop wanted me to take. It was the psychotherapeutic analysis and the ministry with others that gave me a deeper awareness of what it means to know myself.

For most of us this is hard work, and frequently people go through life without ever really coming to know themselves. The sad fact is that as a consequence they really don't come to know God. Notice I say, "to know God." People may come to knowledge about God, but to be in relationship with the unseen deity, that is another matter. As human beings we do not ask for the life that we are living, and though we are the highest order of creation, we are the most helpless of creatures at birth, so helpless in fact that we would not survive without our caregivers, usually our parents. In a spiritual context then, at least as infants, we do not ask for life in God, and generally we are all quite helpless in our spiritual lives. With the help of others, usually our parents and godparents, over time we come into relationship with Jesus Christ. This is a lengthy process, during which we may be led to knowledge "about God," but relationship "with God" is, in my opinion, contingent on love of self, which enables us to love others, which is how we love God.

I came to understand this by first calling to mind the double commandment of love: "You shall love the Lord your God with all your heart, with all your soul, with all your mind, and with all your strength." The second is "You shall love your neighbor as yourself" (Mk 12:30–31). The most meaningful explanation of this I learned is that "we can love God at all only to the extent that we learn to love others, and this whether they deserve to be loved or not."[1] This is remarkable—we love God, by loving other people! During his review of the manuscript that became this book, Father Nigro made this comment: "The precepts of love quoted from Mark in this paragraph are really the old law! The new law of Jesus is Love God as our Abba who lives in us and love one another as I love you." Nigro was saying "Love others together with Jesus in you, loving them." What a wonderful built-in incentive and challenge!

To follow the second precept we can love others only to the extent that we learn to love ourselves, because we cannot give what we don't have! There are various ways of knowing and testing this. One way is by the realization that people generally only compliment in others what they already possess themselves. Another way is by recognizing that in every relation we can either raise or lower the other person in their self-esteem. Our challenge is to affirm others. Unfortunately, many in my generation were taught not to be conceited, nor to think too highly of ourselves, because of the sin of pride. This negative attitude frequently got in the way of loving ourselves. Certainly pride is a sin, but part of knowing ourselves is to respect and love ourselves in a healthy way, because we are wonderfully made and we are basically good, and when we perceive ourselves in this way we are enabled to love others and thus to love God.

I was started on these insights when I entered the seminary, but the foregoing insight evolved more clearly for me during my seminary days. It was a part of my focus with my spiritual director with whom I discussed how to relate to women as a celibate, since my primary way of relating had been as a married man. I wanted to love universally rather than exclusively. I sensed that at times women would take my acts of kindness in a personal way, even though I had not intended this. He concurred with that observation. I did not wish to be rude to women in order to handle my celibacy, as I had observed in some celibate clerics. Initially, I felt that I was coping and growing in the seminary environment. As time progressed, I think my humanness caught up with my idealism. We are creatures of habit, and my twenty-seven years of feminine companionship proved to be poor preparation for me to live as a celibate.

All the while I was learning and growing. My image of God had changed from a judging, punishing God to a loving, compassionate God. My view of the church also changed from an ethereal, hierarchical, structured organization to a human, fallible, and at times unwieldy institution. I came to look upon the magisterium as being analogous to parents in a family setting. I understood how parents endeavor to parent, by instructing, ordering, judging, punishing, and sometimes by ultimatums made and later regretted. I had only begun to learn about the effects of family systems on children. The corollary to this I began to think is that the magisterium's influence on the church system dramatically impacts the faithful—the people of God.

Part of the reason I began to think this is because family system studies are only about fifty years old. In the ten years since leaving the seminary and serving as an ecclesial lay minister in the church, I have reassessed my earlier thoughts in that respect. I came to the conclusion that my story can realistically contribute to a magisterium that has yet to manifest any signs of understanding the effects of the church system upon the people of God. This is deserving of elaboration, which I have deferred to a later chapter, in order to continue the chronology of events.

12

CONTEMPORARY PRIESTHOOD: A DIFFERENT JOB DESCRIPTION

> It is therefore quite clear that all Christians in any state or walk of life are called to the fullness of Christian life and to the perfection of love, and by this holiness a more human manner of life is fostered also in earthly society
>
> *Lumen Gentium*, 40

The theological underpinnings and the pastoral context of the sacrament of orders as it was codified in the Roman Catechism of 1566 and the Code of Canon Law of 1917 were changed during the Second Vatican Council. The new theological and pastoral changes were incorporated into the 1983 Code of Canon Law and the 1992 Catechism of the Catholic Church.

How different was the former ecclesiology? "Ecclesiology" is derived from the Greek *ecclesia* meaning "assembly" and refers to the science or knowledge of the church's nature, purpose, organization, and management. A great illustration of the former ecclesiology suggests that the place of the laity in the church before Vatican II was to sit at the sermon, kneel for communion, and reach into their pockets for the collection: in short, "to pay, pray, and obey!" Extraordinary initiatives by lay people such as Dorothy Day in New York or Pier Giorgio Frassati in Turin were very rare. Altar boys said responses at mass while people often prayed other prayers, because the liturgy was removed, silent, and unintelligible. Books on theology held nothing about the laity. Canon law said the people had one right: to receive spiritual aids from the clergy. This defined the people negatively. Prior to the 1960s, parishes offered mass and the sacraments in Latin, and little more. Converts were quickly instructed; marriage preparation was brief, mainly legal; baptisms except for the careful pouring of water were automatic. The unordained did not enter the sanctuary, prepubescent altar boys were more angelic than human and no ministry connected to the church's life of teaching, liturgy, etc., took place outside of the sanctuary. To conclude this illustration we may say that the parish of 1962 was hardly different from the parish of 962, which was three hundred years before the completion of the Notre Dame Cathedral in Paris and seven hundred years before the Puritans were founding towns in New England.[1]

So what is the basis for the new ecclesiology? Looking first at the Code of Canon Law we find in canon 210: "All the Christian faithful must make an effort, in accord with their own condition, to live a holy life and to promote the growth of the Church and its continual sanctification." This canon was drawn from *Lumen Gentium*, specifically numbers 32, 33, and 40. Canon 211 states: "All the Christian faithful have the duty and the right to work so that the divine message of salvation may increasingly reach the whole of humankind in every age and in every land." One commentary on this canon elaborates thus:

> It is both an obligation and a right for each and every Christian to spread the gospel. This is a universal Christian obligation, binding in all times and in all places until the final coming. It applies not only to Church leaders but to every disciple of the Lord. If the Church is missionary by nature and if all the people of God are the Church, then this obligation and right are but an expression of who we are as Church.
>
> In the 1917 Code, the work of spreading the gospel was primarily the responsibility of the pope and bishops. Others participated in this work by designation from higher authority, and the presumption was that average Christians had a more passive role of supporting the missionary endeavor and of at least not remaining silent when the faith would be endangered if they did so. Otherwise, the task of spreading the gospel was not specifically theirs.[2]

From the 1983 canonical viewpoint, the indelible sacramental character of orders has the following effects:

(a) the ordained person is so configured to Christ that he acts in the person of Christ
(b) the ordained person is distinguished from other nonordained persons among the people of God; and

(c) once validly conferred the sacrament cannot be repeated. There is one sacrament of order. However, there are three grades of order: episcopate, presbyterate, and diaconate. Each level of order has its own responsibilities for the mission of the church.[3]

It is fitting to recall here that two other sacraments carry this "indelible" character such that they cannot be repeated. Those sacraments are baptism and confirmation. Canon 210 bears repeating because it establishes the job description of the nonordained: "All the Christian faithful must make an effort, in accord with their own condition, to live a holy life and to promote the growth of the Church and its continual sanctification." Again, the right and obligation of each Christian is described in Canon 211: "All the Christian faithful have the duty and the right to work so that the divine message of salvation may increasingly reach the whole of humankind in every age and in every land."

From the revised Catechism:

- Having become a member of the Church, the person baptized belongs no longer to himself, but to him who died and rose for us. [1269]
- Incorporated into Christ by Baptism, the person baptized is configured to Christ. [1272]
- Christ, high priest and unique mediator, has made of the Church "a kingdom, priests for his God and Father." The whole community of believers is, as such, priestly. [1546]
- The ministerial or hierarchical priesthood of bishops and priests, and the common priesthood of all the faithful participate, "each in its own proper way, in the one priesthood of Christ." While being "ordered one to another," they differ essentially.[1547]

One recurring theme throughout Vatican II is that the clergy and the laity make up the one people of God and that between them is a mutual relationship of support and dependence, a notion heavily influenced by the Pauline theology of the body of Christ: e.g., ". . . we must grow up in every way into him who is the head, into Christ, from whom the whole body, joined and knit together by every ligament with which it is equipped, as each part is working properly, promotes the body's growth in building itself up in love" (Eph 4:15–16).

The Dogmatic Constitution on the Church (*Lumen Gentium*) introduced this new ecclesiology: a theology of the church as mystery, as the people of God, as the sacrament of the risen Christ and of our salvation. The newness of the ecclesiology was its recovery of older understandings that were lost in the growth and centralization of papal power through the centuries and in the Vatican's defensive response to the Protestant Reformation at the Council of Trent. This newer ecclesiology clashed with the classical Roman theology centered on the pope, the hierarchy, and the church as institution. The two theologies of Church may be visualized by the former ecclesiology as a pyramid with pope, bishops, priests on top, and the nonordained, lay Christians below; and the newer ecclesiology as a large circle consisting of all the baptized with the hierarchy in the center serving rather than dominating the people. This matter was given extensive consideration at the council inasmuch as the first draft of the Dogmatic Constitution on the Church was completely rewritten, the second draft received four thousand amendments, and a thoroughly rewritten third draft was voted on chapter by chapter. Chapter three dealing with the hierarchical structure of the church was voted on article by article. The complete document with its eight chapters received its final vote on November 21, 1964, and was approved with 2151 positive votes and only 5 negative votes.[4]

From this background it is easy to see that the roles of the priesthood and of the laity were significantly changed. Formerly, the priest and nuns did it all. This major change on the part of the baptized is only beginning to be understood by the church at large.

> In a people centered Church rather than a priest centered Church, the priest exercises one ministry among other ministries. The priest functions as servant of God's people in cooperation with and interdependent upon other diverse ministries, less solitary, more communal and as much diaconal as sacral.[5]

In my view, whereas the priest formerly derived satisfaction directly from his mediation, acting as a kind of telephone for God, he must now facilitate an expanded mediation, acting as a system overseer for numerous agents of mediation much like a network server, deriving satisfaction through the cumulative efforts and achievement through many other ministers. Over the past thirty years, the role of the ordained has continued to emerge and evolve. It calls for additional training in people skills, involving the psychology and dynamics of collaborative planning, goal setting, and participatory management. This training is available, and except for individual instances it has generally neither been pursued nor uniformly provided. Another dimension of the emerging role is posed by Donald Cozzens who points out that in the past the priest prayed in order to preach, whereas it may now be claimed that the priest preaches in order to pray. The emerging spirituality of the diocesan priest can be viewed as a dialectical spirituality rooted in his life of faith and prayer, at the same time being forged and shaped through the exercise of his ministerial priesthood.[6]

A further reversal of the theory underlying the 1917 Code is that there are not two kinds of holiness in the church, a higher kind for clergy and a lesser one for laity. There is one common calling to perfection (*Lumen Gentium*, 40). The 1917 Code held that clergy and, by extension, religious were called to live holier lives than lay persons (canons 124 and 592). The revised code accurately reflects the position of the council, that is, whatever one's condition in life, the same holiness is to be pursued in it as in any other situation in life (*Lumen Gentium*, 41).[7]

The foregoing changes are immensely significant. They are not generally known and understood by the people of God nor promoted by the clergy. They are part of the crises of the ordained priesthood described earlier in chapter 10, because they cause confusion and feelings of loss of identity on the part of some of the clergy.[8]

This major change affecting all of the baptized is beginning to take shape in the church at large, buoyed along by the endemic shortage of ordained priests following the major exodus of priests since the council and the reluctance of young men to step forward for ordination. Since we are all called into ministry, it is proper to differentiate between "ministry" and "ordained ministry." They are ministries with different job descriptions. To say this is not to denigrate the former understanding of the ordained ministry, rather it is a call to greater awareness of the responsibility of all of the baptized. We are all called to be Christ bearers—to be Christ for one another.

When Pope Paul VI abolished the minor orders as described in chapter 8, ministries replaced two of the former minor orders and the conferral of ministries was called installation, not ordination. Those two are the office of lector (or reader) and acolyte. The aim of this change was to allow the distinction between clergy and laity to emerge with greater clarity. As such these ministries were limited to men and these installations are an integral part of the process leading to male ordination. However, most local churches (dioceses) have avoided ministries in the sense of that document and have substituted analogous rites for installing men and women to fulfill the functions of the offices of lector and acolyte. This has resulted largely from canon 208, which established the equality of all the baptized. Canon 230 allows for laypersons to carry out certain formerly "priestly" offices.[9]

In 1980, in a parish in a suburb of Edmonton, Canada, a contingent of men and women were trained to be acolytes. They wore albs and served at each of the weekly communal eucharistic celebrations. They had begun a wonderful ministry and the acolytes gathered in the sacristy before mass and prayed together, and became an inspiration for the community. Soon, however, the pastor disrupted the group, on account of the original intent that it be a male-only ministry. I recall this now, because my daughters were seventeen at the time and Monica brought this up at the dinner table and was very upset because of the injustice of this exclusion of women. As has been the case throughout history, those women acquiesced in the face of this injustice, only to be reinstated within a couple of years when women acolytes began serving in other parishes. There is no way that the universal church could ever go back on the practice of installing women as well as men to serve in these ministries. This is a clear example where praxis is shaping our tradition. Praxis, I suggest, is the integration of belief with behavior.

At the time Monica raised this issue I was not particularly empathetic. I had long accepted the traditional patriarchal mentality, and so it didn't occur to me at that time just how deeply Monica felt about this subordination of women. I don't think I commented much one way or the other, but chances are I would have been supportive of the pastor. I don't recall any marked response from anyone else in the family. I am proud of Monica for her keen sense of justice that manifested itself some twenty years ago and for her courage to take a stand. I think that her mother, who was quite pragmatic at times, was a positive influence for Monica in matters such as this.

Much has occurred in my understanding of church since 1980, and I now realize that the changes that were affecting the ministry of acolyte were happening in ministry in general. I now look upon the Second Vatican Council as a major corrective that was in fact building long before the council was called. In his book on ministry, Thomas O'Meara quotes from the writings of Yves Congar. Evidently, Congar did not think that the upheavals that have taken place since the council had their roots in

Vatican II, but in the constrictive decades or centuries before Vatican II. According to Congar, a crisis would have come anyway and the council merely assisted its entry into the church by ending the isolation of the church and giving a wider audience to the church. Congar linked the present time in the church to the gigantic changes touching on culture and the ways of life in society around the world. He felt the things that preoccupy the church today were already present or beginning to appear in the 1950s and even as far back as the 1930s.[10]

For many in the church, the call for an ecumenical council in 1959 seemed questionable. The church appeared to be running well, seminaries were full, Catholic schools were humming, and the church was well supplied with vowed religious serving as teachers and catechists. When the council opened in 1962, Pope John XXIII evidenced surprise himself at having called the council, revealing the influence of the Holy Spirit operating through Giuseppe Roncalli.

Eugene Kennedy has a descriptive parallel to Congar's view that a necessary corrective was beginning to manifest even in the 1930s. Kennedy writes about the famous "red train" that was carrying East Coast prelates and the apostolic delegate across the country to the Eucharistic Congress in Chicago in 1926. In each city the scarlet-robed princes appeared to receive the cheers of the Catholic people who gathered proudly at the train stations for their blessing. Kennedy describes the church of that day as culture one—the institutional church that religion reporters cover as if it were the whole church. He describes culture two as "Tomorrow's Catholics," who don't even look up anymore when they hear the whistle blow because they are too involved in expressing their lives of faith through their work and family. He concludes by suggesting that the more church leaders look to the past in an effort to restore outmoded hierarchical forms, the more they accelerate the collapse of the crimson-trimmed steam train of a bygone era.[11]

Not too long after the council, in the Edmonton archdiocese at least, it was generally talked about and understood that "priests wanted to get off the pedestal." The idea was that their role or office was to take on a new dimension. From time to time, clerics dressed in secular clothing, often with a shirt and tie rather than the Roman collar. As time progressed, depending on the individual priest, many people called them by their first name. More common was the use of a friendlier "Father Mike" rather than "Father Smith." Not everybody understood the full ramification of "getting off the pedestal." I know I didn't really understand it, except that it seemed the priest was to be more of a brother than a father.

More recently when I had the opportunity to view a video of Mary Collins, O.S.B., speaking to the 1998 chapter of her order of Benedictines, I came to a deeper awareness of what was envisioned by the council—or perhaps what we have come to realize about the church, the people of God. Very briefly, Collins identified the historic reality of sacral persons that has always existed in every generation. (See chapter 2 in which I referred to the three priesthoods, Christian, Jewish, and pagan.) The Catholic priesthood was of a sacerdotal nature, that is, the holy man calling Jesus to be present on the altar. The priest offered the Holy Sacrifice of the mass as "another Christ" so that the people could receive the sacrament of Holy Communion or Eucharist. In that theology the focus was on consumption and adoration of the Eucharist. It seems to me that even the term "celebrant" refers to the sacerdotal office. The revised theology of Eucharist has as its focus the transformation of the people of God, to become Christ for others in carrying out the church's mission to the world.[12]

Looking at Eucharist in this way gives greater meaning to the priesthood of all the baptized. It gives greater meaning to the church's mission when we view the church neither as the hierarchy nor the buildings, but as the people of God. The sacerdotal role is thus not "above" the priesthood of all the baptized. Rather it places the priest within the assembly. Church doesn't start with the priest. It starts with God's people. We are the church. The priest is not the celebrant. It is not usual or normal for a lot of people to stand around watching one person "celebrate." We all celebrate. In the Vatican II corrective, the priest is the presider, the table minister, and the leader of prayer for this communal celebration. Six years after the council, the 1971 World Synod of Bishops more clearly enunciated the church's mission to the world in their landmark statement: "The pursuit of justice and the transformation of the world is a constitutive dimension of the proclamation of the Gospel."

Collins in her video adroitly says we should not be surprised that the sacerdotal concept will not give way easily. It is the sacral role reserved to the ordained priest, and although they are aware that it is changing, they are not sure where it will lead, so they hold on to what is known.[13] From my observation, it is a tradition that has been built up for centuries. It is entrenched in the minds and hearts of those who embraced it and by those who were taught that it was the preeminent function in the church.

Regarding ministry, O'Meara comments: "After a long period of overemphasis upon sacrificial Eucharist and sacral priesthood, baptism was given a new appreciation. Baptism made the Christian, but baptism raised the issue of a universal ministry incumbent upon all the baptized." O'Meara elaborates that, contrary to the medieval position, the bishop is no longer defined as a venerable or glorious version of a priest. Rather he is ordained to be the leader of a local church or diocese. The priest is ordained as a presbyter to assist the bishop. The ministry of deacon was restored so that even married laymen were ordained to a ministry to assist the bishop, but a ministry that was not the priesthood. Bishop, presbyter, and deacon each have their own identity, ordination, and purpose. In effect, the statement of the council was saying there is more than one ministry in the church, that not all ministries are ordained ministries, and that ministry is not necessarily joined to celibacy.[14]

We know from the New Testament that there were women deacons ministering in the house churches in the earliest days of Christianity, even as table ministers. Acts records: "while in their homes they broke bread" (2:46b). Aquila and his wife Priscilla are specifically mentioned as instructors in the faith (Acts 18:26). Paul introduces a person in ministry to the Romans: "I commend to you our sister Phoebe, who is a deaconess of the Church of Cenchreae. Please welcome her in the Lord, as saints should. If she needs help in anything, give it to her, for she herself has been of help to many, including myself" (Rom 16:1–2).

O'Meara asks: "Could there be other assistants in the ministry? Other ministers and other ordinations?" He answers as follows:

> The number of Roman Catholics has grown, and the expectation of Church life has expanded. The crisis in the number of priests could not be solved by a greater number of clergy; it touches upon a change within the life of healthy Christian communities. The ministry is both declining and expanding—it all depended upon how you looked at it. There are fewer seminarians but thousands in theological schools; fewer men and women active in parochial schools but many more in social action. The expansion of the ministry is not, then, a random or annoying occurrence but an aspect of a new Church that is comprehending itself anew in its biblical sources and in its commission to be not just Italian or French but worldwide.[15]

Perhaps Tim Unsworth's words bring home like none other the image of the new church. He wrote an article in the July 14, 2000, edition of the *National Catholic Reporter* describing two funeral services. One was for Cardinal John O'Connor, who died in New York in 2000, and the other for Cardinal Joseph Bernardin, who died in Chicago in 1996. O'Connor's funeral recalled the earlier triumphalist liturgies dominated by clergy, ostensibly hundreds of aged prelates in identical chasubles unapologetically clinging to power. Planning was apparently calibrated by clerical thinking reminiscent of another time. Bernardin's funeral he described as a plea for change, calling for recognition of the laity in most aspects of church. That liturgy, planned by Bernardin during his final illness, featured six women pallbearers and a homily by a priest friend rather than a fellow cardinal. In a restaurant window across from the cathedral was a sign that read: "Goodbye, Brother Joseph."[16]

13

ON THE RIGHT TRACK

"Arise, my love, my fair one, and come away; for now the winter is past, the rain is over and gone. The flowers appear on the earth; the time of singing has come, and the voice of the turtledove is heard in our land."

Song of Songs 2:10b–12

The anxiety that commenced in the latter part of the practicum continued for me. I knew I wanted to continue with graduate studies. I decided to return to the seminary in September 1991, looking forward to the retreat and to taking further time to assess my situation. I discussed this with my spiritual director and with Jan, and we came to the point of agreeing not to see one another. In the first week of the fall semester, I was having difficulty getting back into studies after the busy practicum with its attendant stress. I was alerted to two family celebrations in Canada, so I decided to take a week off from studies to be with my family, to share my situation with them, and if possible to meet with the archbishop.

I went to Edmonton and then to Ottawa with my brother for the wedding of our nephew. As it turned out, while I was in Edmonton the archbishop was away and I could not see him. My family visit was helpful, and the change of environment was good for me. I returned from my Canadian visit and began to pick up where I had left off in my classes. Within a week I knew that I wished to keep seeing Jan. I think that my recollection of the "imposed" separation from Irene during our two-year engagement influenced my decision. Today, I understand this was not a denial of the spiritual advice received from Eugene Violini, or of the benefit that flowed from the discernment to remain in the police force.

Rather, it was a decision made in hindsight of the knowledge that Irene only lived until her forty-ninth year and from a lament over the loss of those two years of companionship that might have been, except for an antiquated rule of the police force.

Celibacy as a vocational requirement had impacted me at least temporarily in my first career. Raised social consciousness had eventually led the RCMP to change their policy in relation to marriage. Before it was abolished totally, changes were made so that it was possible to marry with three years service if a member was twenty-one years of age and would accept a transfer to less desirable locations or less desirable duties such as ceremonial duties on Parliament Hill in Ottawa.

It wasn't too long before the policy of the RCMP changed to the point that no waiting period was required. In retrospect, the semimilitary autocratic style of management acquiesced to a respect for the rights of the individual. Improved management strategies virtually eliminated the need for "spur of the moment" personnel transfers. While this is not totally analogous to the church's eight-hundred-year tradition of total celibacy for the ordained, the consequent difficulties that I observed with the former RCMP discipline adds fuel to my perception that God would have the church revisit the question at least in circumstances such as my own. Perhaps this is what was meant in my perceived answer to prayer that I was on the right track.

Attempting to discern the will of God for one's life is not an easy task. The best contemporary insight that I was able to obtain about the will of God came in a discussion with Brother Julius. He shared from his class with Armand Nigro who taught that God always wants the very best for us. In Paul's letter to the Romans, the will of God is described as "what is good and acceptable and perfect" (12:2b). So we try to discern what God's will is for us through prayer, reflection, and spiritual collaboration. Then we make a decision and take action. That process of discernment was not easy for me in 1991, and if anything the task was fraught with vacillation and was probably the most stressful process I have ever experienced.

Word had gotten to Armand Nigro that I wouldn't be returning to the seminary in September, even before I had decided what to do myself. He called me and I met with Armand and told him of the circumstances that gave rise to his receiving this ill-advised information. The effect of this made me recall his earlier remark to me: "Don't come here if you are just trying to find out if you have a vocation. You better know!" I had been quite content with my discernment to go to Mater Dei, and after those three years I didn't feel guilty, but certainly I felt pressure in the midst of my state of wonder, believing I was right to continue my relationship with Jan without fully understanding the events which were unfolding.

On one occasion, Jan and I attended mass together on a Sunday morning at Sacred Heart Parish in Spokane. We were seated near the front and were holding hands, until we noticed that the choir leader had arrived who knew us very well and knew that I was a seminarian. As soon as we saw her, we immediately reacted by simultaneously letting go of each other's hand. This was a surprising reaction from two mature adults, comfortable with showing affection before God, but not comfortable in the face of the expectations of others. This experience gave me some insight into the feelings of how gay people might feel were they to be seen holding hands in a church assembly composed of mostly straight people. What Jan and I experienced was tantamount to the discomfort that outcasts and marginalized people feel. It was weird!

I spoke with the rector and told him that I wished to keep seeing Jan, but since I was in a formation house for celibate living I didn't think it was right. He agreed, pointing out that it wouldn't be good for the reputation of the seminary or for me. A leave of absence was deemed the most appropriate resolution in the circumstances. The rector suggested that I notify my fellow seminarians and the staff as appropriate, prior to my leaving. He also instructed that I not stick around long after making the announcement. This was a difficult instruction to hear. I was being asked to leave quickly, but it felt more like "get out!" I have reflected on that admonition many times since then. I know it wasn't intended for me personally, because the rector also said, "You needn't feel guilty Ron, because you are making a choice between a good and a good, and they are both meritorious."

In my opinion, the admonition to leave soon after making the announcement was given because the mandatory requirement of celibacy is difficult and any potentially undesirable influence upon other seminarians must be minimized. Something is not authentic about this, where men are preparing to make a lifetime commitment that is to be a free response to God in faith. Just as it was not authentic for Jan and me to be holding hands in a "public" forum when I was "publicly" preparing to embrace a celibate lifestyle, so having to safeguard other seminarians from me by having me leave as soon as possible was likewise not authentic. At the very least, it points up the fact that mandatory celibacy is unnatural.

After speaking with the rector, I called the archbishop in Edmonton and asked him for a leave of absence. He was disappointed but gracious and granted the leave, and encouraged me to continue with spiritual direction while I continued with my studies. On October 10, 1991, after evening prayer in the chapel, I announced my decision to my brother seminarians. Each of them embraced me and wished me well. The next day I notified the two staff members. These were difficult emotional experiences for me. My life at Mater Dei had been meaningful and special. I believed I was called to be a priest and I felt accepted in the seminary environment.

I moved out of the seminary on October 12 to my own apartment. I continued with the same curriculum of studies, while the intensity of these events continued to bear down on my life. If I were to embrace marriage with Jan, I could not be ordained. Additional questions arose; for example, what country would I live in? What about my children? What about her children? Where would I work? What of the people that had supported me and encouraged me? I wondered how all this could have happened and at the same time marveled at it. Staying apart from Jan didn't make sense to me. Was this what celibacy was all about I wondered? Was I being weak by responding to the lovableness of Jan?

My continuing studies provided a wonderful opportunity for me to learn about some of the things that I was experiencing. I learned that the extreme anxiety that I had felt in the latter part of the CPE practicum was a principal manifestation of stress. The cause of the stress was the incompatibility of this new relationship with the church's requirement of celibacy. The studies also revealed that stress is most often self-initiated and self-propagated. This led me to think that my decision to seek a leave of absence was positive. I also learned that my vacillating between staying in the seminary and maintaining a companionship with Jan was rooted in loneliness. Loneliness evidently can help a person move toward another human being in spite of anxiety, but not always, for people often endure separation in order to feel and be safe with their habitual self-esteem. In my situation, I was drawn to feminine relationship yet tried to maintain this specific relationship in a state of flux—my need for security forbidding, as it were, a clear commitment. This resulted in a continual testing.[1] When the fall semester ended, I wrote to the archbishop and informed him that I did not expect to return to the seminary in January, but that I would communicate further.

During subsequent graduate classes in pastoral counseling, I came to a deeper knowledge of myself. I learned that grief is the overwhelming convergence of several emotions resulting from loss. The passage of time had allowed me to sort through the pain and conflicting emotions resulting from the loss of my spouse. I came to a clearer, fuller realization that I was missing the feminine companionship that I had known during my marriage. One might think: "Isn't that stupid! Ron needed four years to fully realize that feminine companionship was indispensable to his life!"

In one sense that is true. But in the sense that for over eight centuries priesthood was synonymous with celibacy and that my year of discernment and prayer before entering the seminary affirmed my earlier leanings toward ordained ministry, it was not stupid. Celibacy just went with the territory. It was simply part of my faith tradition. It seemed to me that since I had been married and had children and grandchildren, I would have the best of both worlds. Since I believed that God called me to the ordained priesthood, I responded. My experience of three years and my subsequent discernment caused me to reassess mandatory celibacy. I believed I had a vocation to the ordained priesthood. I gradually came to realize that for me to adhere to the church's policy of mandatory celibacy would be contrary to the natural law and to God's will for me. Heterosexual companionship is normal and natural for me to lead a fulfilling life, especially in ministry. I believe it is wrong for episcopal administrators to insist that I adhere to this antiquated view of human sexuality and thus to conclude that I am not called to the ordained ministry. I began to question compulsory celibacy in relation to God's will for anybody.

During the break at the end of the fall semester, Jan and I went to Calgary where we met with my family who gathered there. The event was complicated by mixed emotions, this new relationship having come up rather quickly, resulting in feelings and expressions of apprehension about where Dad was headed, and minimizing any real manifestation of welcome for Jan.

I resumed my studies on January 15. Jan, meanwhile, had made a commitment to begin her professional ministry with the pastoral care department of a medical center in the Seattle archdiocese. I continued to grow in self-awareness through my classes in theological ethics, theology of ministry, and pastoral counseling. During my spiritual direction with Charlie Skok, he was extremely helpful. His comment to me was: "I am disappointed that you will not be a priest, but I am not disappointed in you!"

I wanted to meet with the archbishop in person and made an appointment to do so on March 12 during the spring break. Meanwhile, I wrote to him and advised him that my discernment had necessarily come down to the point that either I wished to marry, or I wished to be a priest, and since it was not possible to do both I had decided to marry. I informed him that I was comfortable with the decision to marry, but I was not comfortable with the fact that ordination would be ruled out. This and other issues were discussed with the archbishop during an hour-and-a-half meeting, on March 12. I was grateful for his kindness and understanding. He suggested that Jan must be very special, and that he would like to meet her some time. The archbishop agreed to receive a paper that I told him I was preparing. During this brief visit, I chanced upon Duncan MacDonnell who was quite concerned about my change of plans, but in his unassuming way he mostly listened and nodded with what I took to include a disappointing shaking of his head. Later when I saw a younger Edmonton priest whom I had known previously, an angry look and a cold silence met me, not even a greeting. I knew that that kind of judgmental response was his problem, but I felt hurt. That response is wrong because it denies the personal integrity and right of a person to make a free response to God in faith. Christians are particularly adept at making a judgmental response to others in all kinds of situations. It reminds one of Mahatma Gandhi's comment years ago: "Christianity would be all right if it weren't for the Christians!"

While in Edmonton to see Archbishop MacNeil, I received word from Eugene Violini's brother that Eugene had passed away. I was invited to proclaim one of the readings at the funeral to be held in St. Mary's Cathedral in Calgary the next day. I had known of Eugene's fragile health and had wondered from time to time when the end might come and whether I would be able to attend. The timing was coincidental but uncanny that Eugene's end would take place when I was already in Canada, talking to the archbishop of Edmonton about the impasse of my call to ordination. There was consolation for me to have the honor to be a lector at the eucharistic celebration of his life, to see Eugene wearing his chasuble in the coffin, surrounded by hundreds who came to celebrate a life that had so impacted mine. Another judgmental experience ensued. I walked into the hall where the reception was being held after the funeral, and a wonderful younger friend of mine reacted much like the younger priest in Edmonton. Even though I hadn't seen this person for three years, there was no greeting, only a cold silent look of disapproval.

This was another response that I collected and put into the back of my mind, as I struggled to understand the new reality I was dealing with.

Returning to Gonzaga University, I continued to study and ponder the events that had taken place. We hear it said that "God's ways are not our ways," and also "God is a God of surprise." These sayings were very applicable in my circumstances. I came to understand that Armand's admonition "you better know" was made using the term "vocation" to mean inclusively "a call to the ordained ministry and to celibacy." I continued to believe that I was called to the ordained ministry, and in light of the events of the preceding summer I researched the church's tradition of celibacy to try to understand why my perceived call should mandate that I be celibate.

I learned that this "dual understanding" of vocation is in fact a misunderstanding. This was clarified by two documents identified in chapter 8, both of which state that celibacy is not required by the nature of priesthood itself. In the course of my graduate studies, I learned about social systems in which "consensus realities" develop, which ultimately become unconscious. Families and organizations take on these realities and they become systems where the whole is greater than the parts. In these systems, there are rules that if left unchallenged render the system closed, and such closed systems can go on for generations.[2]

Throughout my life in the church, the natural law was constantly used to support church teachings in relation to birth control. Since I contend that the church's tradition of celibacy is an "unnatural law," some clarification of "natural law" is in order. In my studies I came to realize that natural law is the unwritten law of our being. It has not always been understood in the same sense in every age. It is unformulated, thus has no "letter" and is all "spirit." Although it is unwritten, we can ascribe to it a main principle and three subprinciples to aid in our understanding of its spirit. The first principle is "Do good and avoid evil." This principle, of course, does not identify the good to be done or the evil to be avoided. Its subprinciples may be identified as follows: "Preserve your being," "Care for your offspring," and "Avoid alienating those among whom you must live and work." A concept of the natural law was recognized and applied following the Second World War for "crimes against humanity." More recently there have been attempts universally to criminalize these crimes. Suffice it to say here that a more universal awareness of natural law has historical precedence. Any consideration of natural law must also take natural rights into account. We need not prove that there are natural rights, for no one denies this. To deny all rights would require denying all law. If there were no natural law, there could be no natural rights, because there would be nothing to oblige people to respect such rights. Clearly natural law comes from our capacity to reason. St. Thomas Aquinas in his twelfth-century *Summa Theologica* argued to the existence of an eternal law based on divine reason, the notion of which has the nature of a law.[3] Christians seeking to connect the temporal natural law to the eternal "ordinance" of divine reason establishing order and harmony in creation for the common good can look to Scripture:

> For when the Gentiles who do not have the law by nature observe the prescriptions of the law, they are a law for themselves even though they do not have the law. They show that the demands of the law are written in their hearts, while their conscience also bears witness and their conflicting thoughts accuse or even defend them on the day when, according to my gospel, God will judge people's hidden works through Christ Jesus. (Rom 2: 14–15)

The church's centuries-old tradition of celibacy became a "consensus reality" that is unconscious. This unconscious reality is a façade because it is compulsory. Like "arranged" marriages of old, "compulsory" celibacy could become authentic, but its imposition is an affront to the dignity of a candidate for ordination and a denial of his right to a free response to God in faith. The Vatican Council Declaration on Religious Freedom puts it this way:

> It is ***in accordance with their dignity*** [emphasis added] that all men, because they are persons, that is, beings endowed with reason and free will and therefore bearing personal responsibility, are both impelled by their nature and bound by a moral obligation to seek the truth, especially religious truth. They are also bound to adhere to the truth once they come to know it and direct their whole lives in accordance with the demands of truth. But men cannot satisfy this obligation in a way that is in keeping with their own nature unless they enjoy both psychological freedom and immunity from external coercion. Therefore ***the right to religious freedom has its foundation not in the subjective attitude of the individual*** but ***in his very nature*** [emphasis added]. For this reason the right to this immunity continues to exist even in those who do not live up to their obligation of seeking the truth and adhering to it. The exercise of this right cannot be interfered with as long as the just requirements of public order are observed.[4]

Having arrived at this impasse with the institutional church, I continued my research and my discernment, doing what I believed in conscience was right and was open to me, namely, opting for marriage. While in the seminary I prayed for the grace to be a good priest, and if I couldn't be a "good priest" then I didn't wish to be a priest at all! The meaning, which I believe I was assigning to "good," had to do with fulfilling all the obligations that I would accept at ordination. I think the only obligation that in my subconscious was an "unknown" was how difficult the rule of celibacy might become for me. One thing I did know was that I was instinctively attracted to women. Remarriage was not something I had sought for all the reasons earlier stated. From the experiences that I have described, it can be seen that this concern only progressively began to manifest itself as a potential issue. At the outset I was confident and very happy with where I was and with my sights set on ordination.

I completed all of the studies required of me for ordination, including the ministry class wherein two seminarians and I were taught how to say mass. This was rather difficult since my former brother seminarians and the priest instructor from Gonzaga University knew of my plan to marry and the likelihood that I would not be ordained. Both seminarians have long since been ordained, one in Saskatchewan and the other in Idaho.

Jan and I prepared for my graduation on Saturday, May 9, and we arranged to marry on Sunday, May 10. It was Mother's Day and we were married at St. Joseph's Church in the valley east of Spokane in the presence of our children, Jan's parents, and our friends. Jan's spiritual director and my spiritual director were in the sanctuary. We enjoyed an evening reception at the Cataldo Cafeteria on the Gonzaga Campus. The next day Jan and I left for Seattle and a brief honeymoon in the San Juan Islands. We lived in the apartment where Jan had lived since the end of February and Jan continued to serve as a hospital chaplain while I set about the business of finding work.

This was a time of adjustment for me. I had never experienced unemployment before. I had moved away from Edmonton to a small city in 1981, happy to get away from the traffic. Now I found myself in Seattle with its underdesigned highway system and extensive commutes, trying to find work with a Master of Arts in Pastoral Ministry. Nothing materialized until I was accepted to serve in a part-time role in a Seattle parish. Jan, on the other hand, was happy to be in Seattle near the water. Over time I became more settled and the milder climate from the Canadian below-zero winters was easy to take.

In this first parish I set about doing what was asked of me, but it wasn't too long before a certain tension began to emerge. I had been used to relatively competent management in the RCMP where I learned how to manage and became an instructor of practices of management. In my second career I experienced a highly competent and professional management system. I was thrilled by what I had learned in my four years of schooling about how much the church had kept pace with societal changes and growth. I attended staff meetings in the parish and it soon became apparent that the management style was one that had been learned in the church. It can be described in one word: *control*. Purportedly, it was a Vatican II style, with a "first name approach." But it was devoid of any real participatory or consultative processes. Human relations and communication skills were conspicuous by their absence. The reason for this, I believe, is that seminaries do not teach them. They are skills that must be learned. In situations such as this, when differences of opinion arise, a "control style" resorts to a "power style." I soon became disillusioned. I had taken another part-time position in a retail store to help us meet the high cost of living in Seattle. The best description of what happened to me in my first paid position in ministry is: "I was drummed out." I was devastated by the way I was treated. I resigned before the year was out, having been encouraged to do so without waiting for the end of the fiscal year. I was offered a full-time position in the retail role, but I decided to resign from that position because of the commute and because I was still discerning my future.

Early in my first paid ministry position, the pastor wrote to the archbishop recommending me to be ordained as a married deacon. He told me of this action after the fact and suggested I call the director of the Deacon Program. I tried to alert the pastor to the fact that I did not wish to become a deacon. When the archbishop came to the parish I spoke to him briefly and asked if I could come to see him. He agreed, suggesting I drop him a note to set up a time. After my resignation, I continued to search for work and decided to take training and licensing for a sales role. I was barely started in this activity when I received a call from the pastor of another church in Seattle, where an opening existed for a full-time pastoral associate. With Jan's urging and at the request of the pastor, I interviewed for the position and it was suggested that I give the matter some thought and pray about it and arrange for a further interview. At the second interview, I was informed the position was mine and no further interviews would be required. We discussed my earlier parish experience and this pastor acknowledged that he was not trained in administrative management but assured me there would be "no looking over my shoulder." It seemed to me that this was a more honest approach even though I was still quite apprehensive about paid "lay ministry" from what I had observed in the Seattle archdiocese. Jan and I had met during chaplain training and both of us were motivated to discipleship. Naturally, Jan encouraged me to accept the role and I did so with a renewed sense of discipleship, albeit with some trepidation.

As I began to work into this new role, a new kind of discernment began to emerge. I had not yet gone to see the archbishop as it was not clear in my mind how or what I would ask of him. I knew that it wasn't to be about becoming a deacon. I began to write about priestly ordination as a married man. I sought advice from the priest in this new parish, and he was constructive and helpful. I researched the Code of Canon Law and the more I was involved in ministry and the more I learned about the shortage of priests in the Seattle archdiocese, the more it became clear what I should ask of the archbishop. The Seattle archdiocese held a number of meetings and initiated draft papers during 1994. These culminated in a publication entitled "Pastoral Care of Parish Communities." One item stated: "There is the urgent need now to provide pastoral leadership for parish communities who will not have a resident pastor effective July 1, 1995, as well as in the years ahead."[5]

I learned of a dispensation under canon 1042 of the Code of Canon Law whereby the Holy See may grant permission for a married man to be ordained. Soon I knew why it was that I wanted to see the archbishop. I wrote the archbishop for an appointment, which was granted on a Wednesday afternoon.

I had been working at Mt. Vernon chaperoning young people on a mission project assisting day-care workers for children of Hispanic migrant farm workers. We were housed in a parish building in Mt. Vernon and I got away a bit late, so I was ten or fifteen minutes late in arriving at the bishop's office. I brought with me the following letter. (The attachment, which was a brief synopsis of my autobiography, is not reproduced here.)

Ron Eberley
4807 - 37th Ave. S.W.
Seattle, Wa. 98126
July 20, 1994

The Most Rev. Thomas J. Murphy, D.D.
Archbishop of Seattle
910 Marion Street
Seattle, Wa. 98104

Dear Archbishop Murphy:

Thank you for meeting with me and for receiving this letter and attachment. Please accept this as my formal request to receive the Sacrament of Holy Orders, and for the necessary dispensation from Canon 1042 by the Holy See because I am married.

Please also accept this letter as a response to your February 1994 letter and draft document relating to the Pastoral Care of Parish Communities.

When making this request I rely upon Canon 213 which identifies the right of the faithful to receive assistance out of the spiritual goods of the church, including the sacraments, and the fact that this dispensation has been granted at various times in the history of the church.

I present myself to you and to the Holy See, with a focus on the sufficiency and availability of Holy Eucharist, considering the needs of Parish Communities in Western Washington. My Pastor Fr. Thomas Quinn is aware of this reqest. I encourage your consultation with him and I look forward to further discussion with you. May God bless you and bring you to a favorable response to this request.

Sincerely in the mystery,
and the awesome love of Christ,

Ron Eberley.

The Archbishop sent me the following reply:

ARCHDIOCESE OF SEATTLE
910 MARION STREET
SEATTLE, WASHINGTON 98104-1299
(206) 382-4375
FAX (206) 382-3495

OFFICE OF THE ARCHBISHOP

August 19, 1994

Mr. Ron Eberley
4807 37th Avenue SW
Seattle, WA 98126

Dear Ron,

I appreciated your visiting with me at the end of July. I have read several times the document that you left with me. Your life and history are indeed an interesting story. However, in light of the present law of the Church, I cannot accept your request to seek a dispensation from Canon 1042 by the Holy See. Moreover, according to Canon 1047, 2, #3, this impediment is reserved to the Holy See.

Ordination, as you know, is a call by the Church through the Bishop to serve God's people. It is not a vocation one assumes oneself as a result of a personal call. Ordination to priesthood only happens after a Bishop has known the candidate for a number of years and is convinced that the seminary preparation, spiritual life and personal qualities will enable the candidate to be an effective priest.

I pray that your ministry at Our Lady of Fatima may be a life-giving and energizing experience for you.

Sincerely yours,

Thomas J. Murphy
Archbishop of Seattle

I was disappointed but I had supposed from our conversation that this was likely to be the response. In the months that followed I met with Bishop Skylstad in Spokane who had received me in the ministry of lector while I was still in the seminary. He indicated he would speak with Archbishop Murphy about my desire for ordination.

All the while that my hope kept up and my contacts with bishops were ongoing, I continued to serve as a pastoral associate in the parish. Jan continued to work as a chaplain on the oncology floor of a major hospital in Seattle. Sometimes I attended functions associated with her colleagues, and quite regularly Jan assisted me with ministry in the parish, notably as coanimator for the Rite of Christian Initiation of Adults. This was great, except that it was difficult for Jan to do this over and above her full-time role as a chaplain. In the summer of 1995, an opening for a lay minister occurred in the parish where I was working, and during a discussion with the pastor about filling this position he suggested I ask Jan to give him a call. Jan did so, went to an interview, was hired, and became a pastoral associate alongside of me in the same parish. This was something that neither of us had really anticipated but seemed to be an answer to my earlier request of the archbishop that Jan and I might have the care of a community. Not that the archbishop had anything to do with Jan's appointment, but at least here was an opportunity to be in ministry together.

I wrote to Archbishop MacNeil in Edmonton and to Bishop Paul O'Byrne in Calgary and to the bishop in St. Paul, Alberta, who had been so hospitable to me. I decided to write Archbishop Murphy again, and it was difficult getting a response so I sent the following request:

Ron Eberley
4807 - 37th Ave. S.W.
Seattle, Wa. 98126
Oct 24th, 1995

The Most Rev. Thomas J. Murphy, D.D.
Archbishop of Seattle
910 Marion Street
Seattle, Wa. 98104

Dear Archbishop Murphy:

Thank you for your reply to my letter of Feb. 14th which you copied to Fr. George Thomas and John Reid.

To this date however, I have not received a reply to my letter of Feb. 2nd, relating to my aspiration for priestly ordination.

I have talked with John Reid, and have met with Fr. Thomas concerning the eligibility of Jan and me to assist with the pastoral care of a faith community. I am concerned now that my request through you, to seek a dispensation that is reserved to the Holy See, has been detrimental.
I would appreciate an opportunity to speak with you so that we may come to know one another better, and hopefully to clarify my situation.

I have now been in professional ministry in the Seattle Archdiocese for more than three years. I have only had one brief meeting with you. There has been a change in how Jan and I continue to serve the Archdiocese, and I have some further information which I wish to present to you.

My apprehensions are not like those of Jeremiah who said "I know not how to speak; I am too young!" But I do ask as Jeremiah did, "Why is my pain continuous, my wound incurable, refusing to be healed?"

May I please meet with you? I can be reached by telephone at O.L. of Fatima 283-1456 or at my home 937-0295.

Blessings and peace,

Ron Eberley.

A telephone response came from the archbishop's secretary and a time was set for a second meeting. That meeting was much different than I had ever imagined it would be. Quite soon after I arrived the archbishop began to become irritated that I was not accepting the response in his letter. He began to be more forceful in his words and eventually told me that if the Vatican authorized him to ordain married men tomorrow, he wouldn't choose me because there were many men who were better than I. I was shocked and began to cry. The archbishop seemed adamant and muttered, "That's OK, that's OK," as if to justify what was happening. I took hold of myself and asked the archbishop how he could say such a thing to me when he didn't even know me. Our meeting lasted the better part of an hour and for most of that time it was a rather tense, challenging, questioning kind of confrontation during which the archbishop pressed me and I responded in a similar fashion. I asked the archbishop many things. I wondered what there was about Jan that now rendered me ineligible for ordination. I told him that in my view that was an oppression of women and the church of my heritage was now oppressing me. I had a copy of a letter from the archbishop of Edmonton in which he offered to add his recommendation to either Archbishop Murphy's or Bishop Skylstad's recommendation. Archbishop Murphy's response was "Let him send it!"

He had been clear that he was not willing to recommend me, and by this time I was both incensed and hurt by his rebuke and our conversation came to an abrupt end after I pointed out that I knew how he thought, but since he could not grant the dispensation I wanted him to send it to the Vatican, and if they said "no," then I would back off. Silence ensued for several minutes. I didn't dare say a word. It was like trying to make a sale. The first one that talks after the presentation loses! Finally, the archbishop spoke in a somewhat conciliatory tone and said, "I'll tell you what. You pray about this and I'll pray about it and I will be going to the Priest Days and after that you come back and see me. And bring your wife—women have a way of settling things down."

More time passed and I wrote again and the archbishop met with Jan and me. He was quite congenial this time, even to the point of saying that I could hardly blame him, because he couldn't in conscience recommend anybody for ordination unless he really knew the person. More time passed and after each meeting with the archbishop I wrote to him summarizing our discussion and offering further elaboration about the issues raised during the meeting.

One would think that the partial realization of Jan's and my goal of our being in ministry together would have enhanced our lives. This was not to be. I received a letter from Bishop Skylstad confirming that he had contacted Archbishop Murphy and explaining that there was no way that my request would be honored by the Vatican and in effect dissuading me from pursuing this matter further.

Archbishop Murphy became ill and was diagnosed with leukemia. This was very sad for the archdiocese. Jan and I were at the hospital where the archbishop was one afternoon and we stopped in to see him, but he was out. While we were arranging to leave some flowers, he came down the hall in a wheelchair pushed by a tall young priest. The archbishop was wearing a surgical mask to protect him in his immune suppressed condition. As he got closer he called out, "Hi Ron, I had a pass!" His aide did not stop but wheeled him right past Jan and me. I was elated by his recognition of me.

The archbishop recovered somewhat by the spring, and I spoke with him briefly when I was at the cathedral with members of our catechumenate for the Rite of Election. I asked if I could come to see him once again, and he told me he hadn't returned to work full-time yet and asked me to wait about a month or so and then give him a call. I waited and watched as the archbishop kept a fairly rigorous schedule making the rounds for confirmation. He came to our parish in May and gave an impressive homily. He was tired but seemed inspired, and I waited until after Easter before sending him a brief note. I know he received the note but there was not time for him to respond. He went to the Priest Days and left on a Thursday evening to attend the National Conference of Bishops but became quite ill en route. He was returned to Seattle where he died the next day.

Months elapsed after the passing of Archbishop Murphy until his successor was appointed. At the banquet held in conjunction with the installation of the new archbishop, I approached Cardinal Mahony who was visiting from Los Angeles. The brief discussion I had with him ended with his suggestion that I send him something in writing.

A copy of my letter to the cardinal and his response are reproduced here:

Ron Eberley
10203 - 47th Ave. S.W. #D-3
Seattle, Wa. 98146-1025
January 12th, 1998

His Eminence
Roger Cardinal Mahony, D.D.
1531 W 9th Street
Los Angeles, CA 90015-1194

Dear Cardinal Mahony:

Thank you for inviting me to write to you, when I approached you briefly at the installation banquet in Seattle on December 18th last. Please forgive my unusual if not impetuous approach.

I believed that God called me to the ordained ministry ten years ago when I responded by entering the seminary in Spokane, Washington under the sponsorship of Archbishop Joseph N. MacNeil of Edmonton, Alberta, Canada. Since that time my life has taken various turns in which I sense the providence of God, impelling me amid much personal stress through prayer, counselling and discernment, to pursue ordination as a married man. I look upon you as the Primate for the Western United States, and thus a person of hope in my response to our God of love.

Enclosed with this letter is an attachment intended to serve as a resume and background summary of events which led me to approach you. I trust that this communication will enable you to understand why I approached you on December 18th.

Upon the death of Archbishop Murphy I felt abandoned--even rejected, realizing that ultimately a new Ordinary would have to be the one to receive my renewed request, which would take additional, valuable time. I rejoice at the installation of Archbishop Brunett. However, I realize that he will require a period of time to become oriented in his new duties before he would be able to consider my request. The issue which my request raises was evidently difficult for Archbishop Murphy, and I can only forsee additional delay due to the transition period. For this reason I appeal to your objectivity and leadership to consider the circumstances of my request, the needs of the Church at this time in history, and their relationship to the building up of the body of Christ.

For more than five years Seattle has been mission territory for Jan and me after having left our children and grandchildren. We are part of the developing Vatican II church, collaborating to introduce love and justice into society. Would you please espouse my application for a dispensation from the Holy See that I may be ordained as a married man? I am willing to travel to Los Angeles to meet with you personally, if necessary.

In the peace and love of Christ,

Ron Eberley

Archdiocese of Los Angeles   Office of the Archbishop   3424 Wilshire Boulevard   Los Angeles California 90010-2241

February 5, 1998

Mr. Ron Eberley
10203 - 47th Ave., S.W., #D-3
Seattle, WA 98146-1025

Dear Mr. Eberley:

I have received your letter of January 29, 1998 in which you describe your personal life and situation.

There is really nothing that I can do here in the Archdiocese of Los Angeles to assist you in the goals which you have set.

With every best wish, I am

Sincerely yours in Christ,

+ *Roger Card. Mahony*
His Eminence
Cardinal Roger Mahony
Archbishop of Los Angeles

eb

Jan and I continued to be in ministry in the parish through a variety of ups and downs and many long days, amidst assorted tensions associated with the lack of administrative leadership. One of the things I experienced was the opposite of "control." That led me to comment to the pastor that I appreciated his "not looking over my shoulder," but that I needed him to look me in the eye and tell me how I'd done! Aside from the commitment and hours worked, parish lay ecclesial ministry is difficult because we frequently have to deal with the deep-seated values of parishioners. The renewal initiated by the Second Vatican Council has been stalled in a number of ways. The church is always in need of renewal, and in this time of transition with a multitude of problems that are not going away, parish ministry is extremely challenging. It must surely have been so for Jesus during his public ministry. That is what has kept Jan and me going. I decided to write to the new archbishop, without which my story would be incomplete.

October 6th, 1998

The Most Rev. Alexander J. Brunett
Archbishop of Seattle
910 Marion Street
Seattle, Wa. 98104

Dear Archbishop Brunett:

It is now ten months since your installation as our Archbishop, and four months since Jan and I accompanied you on the tour to Italy and the Palium ceremony. We will always be grateful for your invitation.

I am writing to you at this time because I continue to recognize signs that I am called to the ordained ministry. I have been very frustrated but feel impelled to press on to whatever God would have me do towards the building up of the kingdom.

This letter is a follow up to a series of letters which I sent to Archbishop Murphy, beginning in July 1994. I mention this because my prior letters may still be on file in your office, and they would afford you some insight prior to your meeting with me.

For the past five years I have served as a Pastoral Associate at Our Lady of Fatima Church. In the course of this experience I have come to a new place in my discernment, but I need to discuss this with you, since as my Ordinary, your views are key to any resolve.

Fr. Quinn and I have discussed my aspirations and preparation for Orders, and the availability or otherwise of the Diaconate at the present time. He suggested that I continue to pray about this and that I write to you. May I please have an appointment to meet with you on this important matter? I may be contacted by telephone (283-1456).

In the peace and love of Christ,

Ron Eberley,
Pastoral Associate.

Much to my disappointment, the following reply seemed to preclude an opportunity of meeting with the archbishop:

OFFICE OF THE
ARCHBISHOP

ARCHDIOCESE OF SEATTLE
910 Marion Street
Seattle WA 98104-1299
Tel: (206) 382-4375
Fax: (206) 382-3495

October 19, 1998

Mr. Ron Eberley
Our Lady of Fatima Church
3307 W. Dravus St.
Seattle, WA 98199-2624

Dear Ron:

I am writing to acknowledge receipt of your letter dated October 6, 1998, in which you express interest in the Permanent Diaconate in the Archdiocese of Seattle. The Diaconate program is currently in the planning stages and will require both my approval and that of the National Conference of Catholic Bishops before applications for the programs are considered.

I will transfer your letter to the office of the Permanent Diaconate and keep it on file during the time the program is being formed. I advise you to watch *The Catholic Northwest Progress* for an announcement when formal applications for the program are being accepted.

Asking God's abundant blessings on you and Jan, I am

Sincerely yours in Christ,

Most Rev. Alex J. Brunett
Archbishop of Seattle

Not until May 2001 did I visit with Archbishop Brunett in person, when I could raise the question of the ordination of a married man. The archbishop told me he did not need a married priest. I had a follow-up meeting with Archbishop Brunett again in August 2001, during which I told him that I believed that I was called to the presbyterate as a married man. I explained that I was willing to undergo the the challenges of being among the first married men so ordained and that I could make that claim because I had discussed it at length with Jan who would share the challenges with me. The archbishop's response was to the effect that he did not feel that the shortage of priests was any reason to ordain married men because of his work and association with married clergy of other denominations, implying that the freedom of clergy to marry in other churches had not always assured them of sufficient ordained ministers.

At one point the archbishop asserted that my vocation was to be a good husband. He spoke disparagingly of "married men" who feel they are "called" to the priesthood because of the priest shortage. It was clear that I was being included in this abstract group of men of "doubtful call." I found it necessary to remind the archbishop that I had left my children, my home, and my business to enter the seminary in 1988.

At this point in my attempt to follow my conviction of being called to the ordained ministry, I have no alternative but to present the circumstances of this intransigence together with my research to the people of God. I have great confidence in the faith that God instills in people and in their capacity to witness to the truth. Indeed, I call upon the faithful to take a stand and to be Christ for the world in this important matter.

14

THE CALL QUESTIONED: WHY CELIBATE? WHY OBLIGATORY?

> Look, my eye has seen all this,
>   my ear has heard and understood it.
> What you know, I also know.
>   I am not inferior to you.
> But I would speak to the Almighty,
>   and I desire to argue my case with God.
>
> Job 13:1–3

The First Question: Why Celibate?

> Canon 1037—An unmarried candidate for the permanent diaconate and a candidate for the presbyterate is not to be admitted to the order of diaconate unless in a prescribed rite he has assumed publicly before God and the Church the obligation of celibacy or professed perpetual vows in a religious institute.

In chapter 2 reference was made to the fact that very little of the Old Testament cultic practices in relation to the sexual act were carried over into the New Testament. Thus a critical question arises from the New Testament: How can the church allow the force of ancient laws of purity when Jesus and the New Testament writers revoked the ritual precepts of the Old Testament and declared them void? Catholic Church documents down to and including the encyclical *Sacra Virginitas* of Pius XII (1954) have referred to the Levitical laws of purity in connection with priestly celibacy. The primary passages quoted are Ex 19:15; 1 Sam 21:5–7; and Lev 15–17 and 22: 4.[1]

The full council at Vatican II approved two documents that included sections devoted to celibacy. These were the Decree on the Training of Priests (*Optatam Totius*) on October 28, 1965[2] and the Decree on the Ministry and Life of Priests (*Presbyterorum Ordinis*) on December 7,

1965.³ However there was a distinct limitation placed upon the council so that the full council was not given the opportunity to debate and to reassess the entire context of ecclesiastical celibacy. In other words, the collegiality of the world's bishops has not been brought to bear on the central issue of celibacy.

The Decree on the Training of Priests included this passage on celibacy:

> Students who follow the venerable tradition of priestly celibacy as laid down by the holy and permanent regulations of their own rite should be very carefully trained for this state. In it they renounce marriage for the sake of the kingdom of heaven (cf. Mt. 19:12) and hold fast to their Lord with that undivided love which is profoundly in harmony with the New Covenant; they bear witness to the resurrection in a future life (cf. Lk. 20:36) and obtain the most useful assistance towards the constant exercise of that perfect charity by which they can become all things to all men in their priestly ministry. They should keenly realize with what a sense of gratitude they should embrace this state, not only as a precept of ecclesiastical law, but as a precious gift of God which they should ask for humbly and to which they should hasten to respond freely and generously, under the inspiration and with the assistance of the Holy Spirit.
>
> Students should have a proper knowledge of the duties and dignity of Christian marriage, which represents the love which exists between Christ and the Church (cf. Eph. 5:32). **They should recognize the greater excellence of virginity consecrated to Christ, however, so that they may offer themselves to the Lord with fully deliberate and generous choice, and a complete surrender of body and soul.** [Emphasis added]
>
> They should be put on their guard against the dangers which threaten their chastity, especially in present-day society. They should learn how, with suitable natural and supernatural safeguards, to weave their renunciation of marriage into the pattern of their lives, so that not only will their daily conduct and activities suffer no harm from celibacy, but they themselves will acquire greater mastery of mind and body, will grow in maturity and receive greater measure of the blessedness promised by the Gospel.⁴

This decree on the training of priests offered a *new* New Testament basis for celibacy in its reliance on the Gospel of Matthew: "Some are incapable of marriage because they were born so; some, because they were made so by others; some, because they have renounced marriage for the sake of the kingdom of heaven. Whoever can accept this ought to accept it" (Mt 19:12). It would appear that the basis for the historic rulings which underlie celibacy were the socially inherited, apocryphal notions of human sexuality. I use apocryphal in reference to pre-Christian and nonscriptural Christian works. Those inherited notions ostensibly found support in some practices recorded in the Hebrew Scriptures and in many of the earliest Christian churches where sexual abstinence even by married couples was observed in association with their baptism.

The Vatican II Decree on the Training of Priests confirms that the apocryphal and the Hebrew scriptural basis for celibacy no longer hold. Clearly there has been a shift, in effect a retraction of the prior grounds for clerical continence in marriage that led to mandatory celibacy. However, the final sentence of the scriptural passage from Matthew 19 implies that responsibility for the adoption of a celibate lifestyle is personal: to be accepted by those who are capable of accepting that lifestyle. That personal decision is thus denied to all who perceive a call to the ordained ministry and canon law therefore contravenes Matthew 19:12.

A commentary on canon 277 reflects on the change in the grounds for clerical celibacy:

> In this positive presentation, "for the kingdom of heaven," the conciliar statements as well as the revised law are a great improvement. "All untenable motives for celibacy—arising from notions of cultic purity or from a subliminal depreciation of the body and of sexuality—are avoided, motives still commonly mentioned until quite recently in official documents."

A footnote in the same commentary reveals the following:

> Pope Pius XII permitted a group of former Lutheran pastors in Germany who were married to be ordained to the priesthood in the 1950s. In December 1967 Pope Paul VI granted a similar dispensation to several married men in Australia who had been Anglican clergymen. In October 1969 Peter Rushton was ordained by Cardinal Gilroy in Sidney (P. Rushton, "A Married Priest in Australia." (CR 66 [1981], 383–386).[5]

Further commentary relating to canon 277 has this to say:

> The 1917 law (CIC 132) stated that clerics in major orders are barred from marrying and so bound by the obligation of chastity that

if they sin against it they are guilty of sacrilege. The Secretariat, while agreeing that the violation of perfect continence is a sacrilege, relegates that issue to moral theology. In view, however, of the abolition of the "privilege of the canon" (*CIC* 119) which made the physical violation of a cleric or religious a sacrilege (thus with a connotation of cultic purity), it seems more appropriate to refer to the sexual transgressions of celibates not as sacrileges but as violations of a vow. In the past it was controverted whether the obligation of celibacy arose from a vow implicitly taken at the reception of the sub diaconate or from ecclesiastical law. Under the present discipline canon 1037 requires before the reception of the Diaconate a candidate who is not married must, in a prescribed rite, assume publicly before God and the Church the obligation of celibacy—or have made a perpetual vow in a religious institute.

The 1917 Code (*CIC* 132 §3) ruled that a married man who received major orders without an apostolic dispensation, even in good faith, was prohibited from exercising those orders. The revised new Code does not deal with this situation in the canon on celibacy, but in canon 1042, 1° it declares that a man who has a wife, unless he is legitimately destined for the permanent diaconate, is simply impeded from receiving orders; in canon 1044 §2, 1° it states that a person who illegitimately received orders while bound by an impediment is impeded from exercising those orders. Good faith does not enter into consideration. According to canon 1045 ignorance of the irregularities and of the impediments to ordination does not exempt from them.[6]

This commentary illustrates that what was formerly considered sacrilegious now has a lesser culpability: that of breaking a vow. The second aspect of this commentary has relevance to the 1970 ordination of a Czechoslovakian woman, Ludmila Javorova, in the "underground church," who, when the fact of her ordination came to light, ceased her priestly activities at the command of Rome.[7] Truly "good faith does not enter into consideration"!

Not surprisingly, the notion from the Council of Trent that virginity consecrated to Christ is a higher state than the married state was reiterated in the Decree on the Training of Priests. This passage in the October 1965 decree contradicted the new ecclesiology approved earlier in the November 1964 Dogmatic Constitution on the Church (*Lumen Gentium*), which stated that there are not two kinds of holiness in the church, a higher one for clergy and a lesser one for laity. This is incorporated in canon 210 of the 1983 revised Code of Canon Law (see chapter 12). This exemplifies not only the deep entrenchment of clerical celibacy but also the prevailing attitude of superiority over the laity that accompanied it and continues to this day.

Christian doctrine "develops"—a concept that was accepted with the approval of the Declaration on Religious Liberty (*Dignitatis Humanae*) on December 7, 1965, drawing on the work of John Henry Cardinal Newman in his *Essay on the Development of Christian Doctrine* and on the labors of John Courtney Murray discussed at the council.[8] The shift in the grounds for clerical celibacy is an example of the development of doctrine. This collegially accepted principle that doctrine "develops" was redrafted six times before it was finally approved 2308 for and 7 against. Essentially the bishops agreed that Catholic teaching changes by being further "developed." This development occurs through the work of theologians, adaptations to changing historical and social conditions, the response and sense of the people of God over time, and especially through the guidance of the Holy Spirit. The reality and extent of this immensely important document is still being experienced in the church.

The 1965 and 1967 statements of Pope Paul VI and Vatican II making it clear that celibacy is not essential to priesthood dramatically weaken the traditional basis for clerical celibacy. Catholic theological understanding today is that God's people are basically good and are wonderfully made. There is one kind of holiness in the church. It is therefore no longer arguable that sexual abstinence is essential for ritual worship or is necessary and more efficacious as a total lifestyle for priestly ministry. Respect for life tells us that human sexuality is a gift, is personal, is generative, and both Paul (1 Cor 9:5) and Matthew's gospel (19:12) leave the acceptance or nonacceptance of that gift, for any reason whatsoever, up to the individual.

The Second Question: Why Obligatory?

> Canon 277—§1. Clerics are obliged to observe perfect and perpetual continence for the sake of the kingdom of heaven and therefore are obliged to observe celibacy, which is a special gift of God, by which sacred ministers can adhere more easily to Christ with an undivided heart and can more freely dedicate themselves to the service of God and humankind.

Canon 277 is emphatic that a priest is *obliged to observe celibacy*. It appears to have been inserted in the 1983 revised code to be faithful to the tradition established in 1139 at the Second Lateran Council that only the unmarried may serve in the ordained ministry. Today's understanding of celibacy no longer holds the meaning that it may have held in 1139.

In light of the earlier canon law that married clerics were not to send their wives away because not only "continence" but "living together in love" were required (see chapter 2), the ruling of the Second Lateran Council in 1139 that wives were to be separated from their husbands was a contradiction of the earlier ecclesiastical law. In this context, it is significant that canon law itself "developed." During the first ten centuries of the church various collections of ecclesiastical laws existed and sometimes contradicted one another. These were evidently put into order at the private initiative of the monk Gratian. Subsequent efforts were undertaken to regularize and consolidate canon law until ultimately, at the instigation of Pope Pius X, the "universal, exclusive and authentic consolidation" of ecclesiastical laws was promulgated on May 27, 1917, by his successor Benedict XV. This universal Code of Canon Law was revised in 1983 to include the correctives of the Second Vatican Council.

Since the Second Vatican Council updated the theology of marriage from that of a "contract," according to the 1917 Code of Canon Law, to that of a "covenant," affirming the properties of unity and indissolubility, the 1139 ruling separating wives from married clerics would be viewed from the vantage point of the twenty-first century as reprehensible. However, this attempt to adhere to the former tradition could not have been seen during the Second Vatican Council since the details of the council's deliberations took time to be fully assimilated and integrated into the revised laws, rubrics, and rites.

Similarly, we become aware that a twelfth-century papal ruling is contradicted by a separate aspect of the Declaration on Religious Liberty (*Dignitatis Humanae*). During the twelfth-century scholastic reforms when sacramental theology was revised and updated, the radical idea gained ground that marriages of higher clergy could simply be proclaimed "invalid." This removed the new hope of married clerics that sprang from the raising of marriage to the level of a sacrament during these reforms. Gregory VII did not declare that marriages of higher clergy were invalid but treated them as though they were. He forbade attempts to find historical or theological bases for the marriage of priests.[9] This "forbidding" directive, viewed in our contemporary understanding, is also reprehensible.

The more I have pondered this intense hold by male celibate clerics, the more frustrated I have become. It isn't because of the antiquated and pernicious notion that something is dirty or sinful about the expression of human sexuality even in the context of marriage. No. My frustration stems more from the fact that celibacy is still obligatory rather than optional in these enlightened times. A respected theologian and friend, himself a priest for over forty years, expressed the opinion that less than half of the ordained celibate clergy have the charism to be celibate. Another long-time priest who read my manuscript felt that the number of ordained males who do not have the charism to be celibate is closer to 97 percent! He told me that he is against compulsory celibacy because it is "tempting God." "It's as though the church required priests to be seven foot tall and then expected God to provide such candidates." Compulsory celibacy, he said, masks authentic celibacy.

During a visit with a married inactive priest, I mentioned the comment of my theologian friend speaking of less than half of the ordained having the charism to be celibate. The inactive priest immediately responded: "If it is a charism!" This caused me to reflect further on this entire malaise. The idea that celibacy is a charism is a misnomer. In my opinion mandatory celibacy is a deprivation. In 1 Corinthians 12 Paul describes spiritual gifts. He delineates different kinds of spiritual gifts, different forms of service, and different divine "workings," and he identifies manifestations of the Spirit given for some benefit as follows: expression of wisdom, expression of knowledge, mighty deeds, prophesy, discernment of spirits, varieties of tongues, and interpretation of tongues. Not here or anywhere else does Scripture identify celibacy as a spiritual gift. Procreation is the gift. In my view celibacy is a state of life, a way of being, freely chosen. But the discipline of the church in canon 277 says candidates are "obliged to observe celibacy." The pervasive "mandatory-ness" of this discipline is further illustrated:

> Canon 1036—In order to be promoted to the order of diaconate or of presbyterate the candidate is to give to his own bishop or to the competent major superior a signed declaration written in his own hand, testifying that he is about to receive sacred orders of his own accord and freely and that he will devote himself perpetually to the ecclesiastical ministry, this declaration is also to contain his petition for admission to the reception of orders.

This canon too needs to be exposed to the developing light of the 1965 Declaration on Religious Liberty in the sense of how church leaders have invoked disciplinary norms and the "development" of such norms. It takes time for the full ramifications of this remarkable document to be "developed" in all its nuances. It was referred to by Pope Paul VI as "one of the major texts of the Council." This was a truly revolutionary document. Its basis is summarized in this important statement:

> . . . the right to freedom in religious matters, freedom from psychological and external coercion, and freedom to seek truth, embrace it, adhere to it, and act on it inheres in each man and woman by reason of his/her dignity as a person endowed with reason and free will and therefore endowed with conscience and personal responsibility.[10]

Viewing all of this with a twenty-first-century mindset, one asks: "How can mandatory celibacy be freely chosen?" One can choose a spouse. One can choose an occupation or a vocation. But ought a person be ***forced to "choose"*** to be celibate? It would seem that the Declaration on Religious Liberty has answered this question, when the essence of its paragraph 3 was inserted some twenty-seven years later into the Catechism of the Catholic Church:

> 1782. Man has the right to act in conscience and in freedom so as personally to make moral decisions. "He must not be forced to act contrary to his conscience. Nor must he be prevented from acting according to his conscience, **especially in religious matters**." [Emphasis added]
>
> 1788. To this purpose [to choose in accord with conscience], man strives to interpret the data of experience and **the signs of the times** assisted by the virtue of prudence, by the advice of competent people, and by the help of the Holy Spirit and his gifts. [Emphasis added]
>
> 2230. When they become adults, children have the right and duty to **choose their profession and state of life.** [Emphasis added]

Accepting the church's discipline of obligatory celibacy illustrates the goodness and generosity of men sincerely trying to discern the will of God. To discern their call to the ordained ministry they must accept it as both a lifelong commitment and an ***unnatural*** celibate state of life. Why? That the sacrament of orders is "indelible" and never to be repeated does not mean that it has to be practiced "full time" for the rest of a person's life. Society has undergone many changes such that in the contemporary world it is becoming increasingly common for a person to have two or three different careers.

The declaration of 1139 distorted God's gift of human sexuality, making it a burden for more than half of the heterosexually oriented clergy, if we accept that less than half of those admitted to orders have the capacity to be celibate. That a person perceives a call from God to be ordained does not automatically mean that the person ought never to express his sexuality. Every priest, every bishop knows what I mean by "burden." They know the difficulties. In the words of a close priest friend, "They [the people of God] don't really know how hard it is to stick to it." In the words of an elderly monsignor, "It's easier to be a good priest when you are an old priest."

In the gospel of Matthew Jesus accused the Pharisees of nullifying God's word "for the sake of your tradition" (15:6b). This intrusive law of mandatory celibacy in the church has wreaked untold havoc in human relationships to the point where it can no longer be ignored. To date, approximately 23,000 priests have left active ministry in the United States and virtually one hundred thousand worldwide. In the United States there are more "married priests" than institutionally active priests. More than ten percent of U.S. parishes do not have a resident pastor. Worldwide the number is closer to fifty percent without a resident pastor.[11]

The havoc I refer to consists of the broken hearts of thousands upon thousands of couples that severed their relationships so the man could become a priest with its accompanying burden of celibacy. Many thousands of those who decided not to be ordained and thus to forgo their perceived call from God had to work through their struggles. Thousands of priests who left active priesthood in my lifetime—let alone unknown numbers of men who left during the previous eight centuries—also had to work through struggles of guilt and grief due to loss. The havoc also includes other casualties, namely, celibates who failed to remain faithful to their vows by abusing others, whether single or married or children, women victims of illegitimate pregnancies, broken marriages, cover-ups by the church which have wrongly protected clerics, priestly scandals which could not be covered up, and more recently the denying of thousands of former priests the opportunity for even voluntary ministry—ostensibly as "punishment." That this state of affairs has been allowed to continue for so long renders the "discipline" of mandatory celibacy at least suspect, and at worst pharisaical.

During my ecclesial ministry, I assisted people wishing to join the Catholic Church. I endeavored to have two personal interviews with each participant during the process. These have been some of the most profound and heartfelt sharings of my ministry. I recall one woman who told me that she had been in love with a man who cared for her but who abandoned their relationship because he wished to become a priest. As it turned out, her friend never did become a priest, and during the intervening years she married another man.

At other times during my ecclesial ministry, I have been approached by women who were victimized by priests, who shared their stories of victimization and of their reporting to bishops, only to be ignored or to be told that they had been the cause of the problem. Virtually every parish in the world has stories of couples breaking off their relationship when the man became a priest and the woman became a nun. One of the priests in a Canadian parish whom I knew while I was an altar boy impregnated a young woman, who went away to have her baby and subsequently entered the convent. We can only speculate about the loneliness, potential guilt feelings, and lives of sadness in the ways the people of God have had to cope because of this intrusive church law. The Scripture passage used as the epigraph for chapter 10 again comes to mind, "They tie up heavy burdens, hard to bear, and lay them on the shoulders of others; but they themselves are unwilling to lift a finger to move them" (Mt 23:4).

During my three-and-a-half-year seminary training in the United States, the Canadian church was devastated by public revelations of the sex crimes of priests and religious brothers (see chapter 10). During a break from studies, I attended mass in a church in Calgary where the homily included comments about those revelations. When I met with my children in Edmonton, they told me of their pastor's comments during a homily in which he reassured the people he was not homosexual nor a pedophile, yet felt constrained from expressing affection toward their children because of the scandals.

The teachings of our church since the Second Vatican Council (1962–1965) have made it abundantly clear that the church is not the hierarchy or the buildings. The church is really the *ecclesia*—the "called out" people of God. But our episcopal administrators are not listening. I have come forward in the belief that I am called to the ordained ministry. Several clerics have suggested that I should simply go my way and forget about this. That is easy for them to say. It is simply not that easy for me to accept. How do I "know" that I ought to pursue priestly ordination? More precisely, why do I believe that I am called to be a priest? The answers to these questions are between God and me and reside deep within my psyche. I have followed the procedures set out by the church to pursue this calling, but they have led to this impasse. What do I do now? Why do I feel impelled to pursue this calling? Is it disobedience, stubbornness, egotism, or does my lifetime of fidelity to the church, my studies and professional ecclesial ministry experience, and the worldwide shortage of priests have something to say on this matter?

The question "why obligatory?" cannot be left without reference to the church's patriarchal tradition. Is the male celibate hierarchy able to be objective in this matter? Each in his own way has had to accept the church's discipline. But for the men who were "obligated" to choose celibacy, regardless of whether they "chose" or "acquiesced," can they now reassess this mandate at least for others if not for themselves?

I ask this because in separate conversations with different bishops, I mentioned that "a married clergy has to come," and I was struck by the fact that in each instance the bishop replied that they didn't agree with me that it had to come. Why this denial? The only way that God is operative in the world is through people—through all of creation, certainly, but essentially through people. As long as there is a need for a ministry of orders, people will be required, and since there is a dramatic illustration that young men are no longer willing to give fifty years of celibate living to the service of the church, denial needs to be overcome.

When I challenge the centuries-old church discipline of "obligatory celibacy freely chosen," I do not do this disparagingly, for my life in the police force was subject to discipline and I came to the realization that there is freedom in discipline. I know too that regardless of how millions of faithful priests over the centuries came to their acceptance of the discipline of celibacy, they did so courageously and by and large with sincerity.

One observation that helps to explain the rigid hierarchical position is that of Avery Dulles taken from his 1988 book *The Reshaping of Catholicism:* "In every decree of Vatican II the conservatives had succeeded in safeguarding their own special concerns. . . . For example, the *Constitution on the Church*, while encouraging the participation of the laity, kept all real power in the hands of the clergy."[12]

A troubling incident, retroactively if not immediately, confirming the contention that the full College of Bishops was precluded from an open discussion of celibacy, is taken from the 1968 book by "Xavier Rynne," *Vatican Council II*. It reveals that on October 11, 1965, the council was "stunned" by a letter addressed to it by Pope Paul VI and read aloud before the assembled bishops as follows:

> We have learned that certain Fathers intend to discuss the law of ecclesiastical celibacy in the Council as it is observed in the Latin Church. Therefore, without infringing in any way on the right of the Fathers to express themselves, we make known to you our personal opinion which is, that it is not opportune to have a public discussion of this topic, which demands so much prudence and is so important. We not only intend to maintain this ancient, holy and providential law to the extent of our ability, but also to reinforce its observance, calling on all priests of the Latin Church to recognize anew the causes and reasons why this law must be considered most appropriate today, especially today, in helping priests to consecrate all their love completely and generously to Christ in the service of the Church and of souls. If any Father wishes to speak about this matter, he may do so in writing by submitting his observations to the Council Presidency which will transmit them to us."[13]

The advances made through medical science, psychology, and sociology relating to human sexuality bear heavily on this archaic discipline for the contemporary church. There is something wanting with the obligatory nature of this ecclesiastical discipline. It is in urgent need of being revisited by the College of Bishops which is itself still undergoing "development" in its awareness and function, pursuant to the Dogmatic Constitution on the Church (*Lumen Gentium*).

The book *Restoration and Renewal* by Joseph Eagan illustrates how chapter 3 of *Lumen Gentium* offered a well-developed theology of the office of bishops, completing as it were the work begun at the First Vatican Council that had developed a rather full teaching on the bishop of Rome, the pope. The First Vatican Council was abruptly ended when Garibaldi marched on Rome and the bishops were forced to flee. The positive Vatican II teaching on the office of bishops, after much debate and strong opposition, restored a critical balance for church governance.[14]

In one sense, the shortage of celibate males is the voice of the people of God. We are speaking up. Several groups are crying for reform. Why are the pastors of the church not listening? This refusal to listen and the restriction on the world's bishops to act is truly a grave omission. It is time for collaboration, not repression.

16

A SEQUEL

May the God of hope fill you with all joy and peace in believing, so that you may abound in hope by the power of the Holy Spirit.

Romans 15:13

When I first prepared to enter the seminary I never dreamt that I would one day ask for a dispensation to be ordained as a married man. At that time I tried to find support for the notion of celibate priests ministering to married people. For example, I reasoned that a male doctor did not have to bear a child in order to aid a woman in childbirth or a doctor need not suffer certain diseases or accidents in order to help cure or heal individual patients. Despite such cursory reasoning, I now believe that an ordained person ought to "bring something to the table" when ministering with people struggling spiritually in the midst of family life issues. My experience of marriage and parenting, including marriage in an extended family context, has given me a broader knowledge and awareness that unmarried clerics do not possess. A good illustration is the death of a loved one. I have experienced the deaths of both my parents and of my first spouse. However, the loss of Irene was unlike any other experience of loss. It has enabled me to reach out to others in ways I never could without having experienced the loss of intimacy, friendship, support, and shared ideals.

I am aware that our theology can and does change, and that it changes ever so slowly. In fact I believe it is best for the church to be conservative lest it fall for fads and fancies that come along. But this is not about a fad or a fancy. This is about natural law versus no "law." It is about a "discipline" that was both misguided and vindictive in its 1139 promulgation. It was misguided because it taught that it was "unbecoming" for men to "give up to marriage and impurity" when marriage is in fact a gift from the Creator and is in no way "impure." It was vindictive because it intended to make effective the equally "unnatural" sexual abstinence that had been imposed on married clergy for seven hundred years. This is about a forced asceticism far more reaching and pervasive than wearing hair shirts and flagellation. It is fraudulent. For the contemporary church it brings up the rights of the baptized. Indeed, it reminds us that Christ died in the pursuit of truth and justice. It calls all Catholics to take a stand for the well-being of the church.

In retrospect it can be seen that the Council of Trent attempted to deflect the Reformation's challenge to mandatory celibacy by insisting that virginity or celibacy was better and more blessed than marriage—a position refuted by the decrees of the Second Vatican Council. It put in place a system that rigidly adhered to its misguided norms, the perpetuation of which anchored the institution in a quagmire of dysfunctional sexuality. Unable to break loose from those sixteenth-century tenets and to trust in the hopes and positive struggles of the Second Vatican Council, the present leadership of the church has made an institutional return to the past, including a highly centralized authority. The result is a church leadership that is locked in denial and uniform mediocrity, limited to parroting the dictates of its centralized headquarters. Lost are the freedom for its members to live their faith holistically and to search for a true theology of human sexuality that would enable the church to mature to adulthood. Disoriented and waylaid, the contemporary church fumbles along in its morass of sexual crimes and celibate infidelity, paying out millions of dollars in penalties and victim settlements while its emasculated leadership masquerades as powerful but is actually powerless.

I call upon the contemporary church, the people in lieu of the powerless hierarchy, to participate in leadership that will liberate us *and* our leaders. The clear and unmistakable signs of the times are calling for an end to compulsory celibacy. Celibacy is a way of life to be chosen, not a duty to be imposed. No human being has the right to insist that another person live celibately. We need to reassess this tradition and to bring to bear the events of our time. I contend that the cumulative events of our time are revealing the work of the Holy Spirit. The evidence is clear. Compulsory celibacy is unnatural, contrary to the design of God for the people of God, and so overwhelming that it is turning our priests and increasingly our bishops into coconspirators of crimes and cover-ups.

It is becoming increasingly clear that "prayers for vocations" are being answered not by increased numbers of celibate priests but by literally thousands of nonordained men and women who are willing to make ministry their vocation. There are upwards of thirty thousand nonordained ecclesial ministers currently working in the church in the United States and thousands more in some stage of academic preparation for ecclesial ministry. It is reasonable to conclude that there is no shortage of vocations. Rather, I believe that the phenomenon of the priest shortage is God's response to decades of prayers for priestly vocations being answered through the universal priesthood of all the baptized.

To support my asking the pastors of the church to cease imposing celibacy on those called to the ordained ministry, I quote the following insight of Edward Schillebeeckx:

> . . . the constant element in the Church's ministry is always to be found only in specific, historically changing forms. Church order, with its changes, is a very great benefit for Christian communities. In one form or another Church order is part of the specific and essential manifestation of the 'communities of God,' the Church. However, this Church order is not an end in itself. Like ministry, it too is at the service of the apostolic communities built on the gospel and may not be made an end in itself or be absolutized. That is all the more the case because it is evident that at all periods of the Church it is utterly bound up with a specific, conditioned history. At a particular point in history, moreover, certain forms of Church order (and thus also criteria for the admission of ministers), called into being by earlier situations in the Church and in society, come up against their limitations; this can also be demonstrated in sociological terms, even in a 'Church of God.' These limitations can clearly be shown in terms of specific experiences of their shortcomings and faults, in other words, from negative experiences with a particular Church order in changed circumstances. With a shift in the dominant picture of [humankind] and the world, with social and economic changes and a new social and cultural sensibility and set of emotions, a Church order which has grown up through history can in fact hinder and obstruct precisely what in earlier times it was intended to ensure: the building up of a Christian community.[1]

What I am calling for will involve a review of the manifold signs of the times, a true assessment of the priesthood of all believers coupled with an application of our revised theology of the Eucharist. It is my sincere belief that this activity bolstered by prayer will lead our episcopal administrators and the rest of the people of God to an authentic change in our tradition. In particular, I believe that it will lead to the awareness that to perpetuate the mandatory requirement or imposition of celibacy is a failure to love and is therefore sinful.

I know that to challenge an eight-hundred-year tradition in the Catholic Church may seem absurd, but this issue is akin to other major issues in the history of the church. There have been other oppressive, entrenched social systems that the church was slow to act upon. An illustration is the way the church handled the question of slavery—a practice that despite condemnation by individual popes over the centuries took nearly nineteen hundred years to be effectively stopped. Another illustration of "closed systems" that result from "consensus realities"[2] that can go on for generations was the practice of castrating choirboys to keep their soprano voices intact, and using these castrati in the Sistine Chapel choir. This lasted for three hundred years, and during this time some thirty-two popes reigned. Pope Leo XIII finally stopped it. I suppose a medieval mentality rationalized that because the purpose was to worship God, castrating boys was acceptable. The boys might even have been schooled willingly to undergo this procedure. I don't know. But hindsight tells us there were broader theological principles that weighed on this question, and praise be to God, the practice is behind us.

A further, though less realized illustration of a consensus reality is the change in the philosophical and theological perspectives on Christian marriage (see chapter 2). From the time of Augustine in the fourth century, it had always been held that the purpose of marriage was *the procreation and education of offspring.* It wasn't until the Second Vatican Council sixteen centuries later that it was agreed that *the good of the spouses* should rank equal with procreation and education. Cardinal Leger of Montreal and Cardinal Deardon of Detroit were instrumental in bringing this about.

Without elaborating on the two former consensus realities, I would like to enlarge on the impact of the latter one, the marriage tradition. But first it is important to touch on what happens to people and the processes they experience every day at all levels of their being as they attempt to function amid the stresses of a consensus reality. People who strive to function in such "closed" family and organizational systems act in ways that minimize the stress of the consensus reality, that is the reality to which everyone consents. They do so to their own detriment. They become codependent.[3] In the first two mentioned systems, the slaves and the castrati were codependent. Good codependent persons are adept at maintaining and perpetuating situations that should rightfully collapse.

The consensus reality relating to the purpose of Christian marriage can really be seen for what it was only in light of advances in human psychology and sociology. These developments have changed individual family systems in my lifetime. A good illustration of this can be seen in the history of the Catholic people in the Province of Quebec. The Catholic people of Quebec were codependent on the consensus reality of the church's lopsided teaching on the purpose of marriage (the procreation and education of offspring) to the extent that they had very large families. I am speaking about twelve, fifteen, eighteen children, for example. Quebec needn't be the only example, for since I have lived in Seattle I became aware of a former practice whereby the archbishop of Seattle would baptize the twelfth child in a family and present the family with a plaque.

More than likely, societal changes during the last half century were instrumental in the virtual elimination of Seattle families having twelve children. It is, however, a significant change and certainly one that accords more with the "good of the spouses." In my former married life, there were many times when I encountered comments of approval from clerics and nuns, because I had five children. At the heart of that attitude was the judgment that I wasn't using birth control so I was a good Catholic. In the Quebec experience, the social revolution that took place and to some extent is still occurring has seen a marked departure from families with double-digit numbers of children.

These familial examples of a consensus reality are admittedly aspects of complicated issues. Indeed, there were some benefits that helped to perpetuate this closed system. Among the most complicated is our understanding of love. Certainly in these large families, there was a great deal of love. Siblings helped their parents to care for one another, and frequently interaction among siblings had a good effect in the shaping and forming of genuinely good people. Difficulties ensued where individual families evolved into their own "closed systems" because of some additional more dominant stress other than their mere numbers, more often than not some "ism" of one or both parents, such as alcoholism, "workaholism," "rageaholism," etc. One or more older siblings frequently emerged as a surrogate parent and became codependent on the dominant stressor, when stepping in to make things work.

For centuries most parents parented the way their parents parented before them, until deciding something had to change. Family system studies have been able to identify characteristics of the first child, second child, third child, etc., and also have revealed how children are impacted by the "system" in their family of origin. In my first marriage, where we had five children, our second son was born a year and a half to the day after our first son. But fourteen months later his twin sisters were born. There was no way that our second son was able to receive the love and affection that his older brother received or that his twin sisters received. We didn't love him any the less, we just did our best. Our fifth child arrived three years after his twin sisters, and his presence was generally positive for all, and probably made up for some lost affection among the others. But in light of this experience, what would it be like for families three times this size? Surely more than one child could "fall through the cracks" and be "lost in the shuffle."

I have raised the church's teaching concerning the purpose of marriage as a consensus reality, because that is exactly what it became over time. It was based on a faulty or limited interpretation of the natural law and remained for centuries. It is not surprising that in the same century that brought the collapse of the closed system that encumbered the church's doctrine of marriage a raised consciousness of the role of women began to emerge. It was emerging quite separately but was making inroads in many facets of life. What this raised consciousness was beginning to challenge was the oppressive consensus reality of the "closed" patriarchal system. I submit that mandatory celibacy is part of that consensus reality and it is time to open up what has been closed for so long.

It is easy to see how a celibate cleric who never has to get up at night with a sick child could urge certain practices upon married couples, totally oblivious of the ramifications of those practices. I can think of one other critical example besides having twelve children. Parents whose son or daughter was planning to marry outside of the church were told they could not attend the wedding and could not even give a wedding present. Ostensibly this was to avoid condoning the actions of their children. In retrospect, this was monstrous leadership foisted on parents that if followed could irrevocably rupture familial relationships.

We have learned a great deal on our earthly journey, partly by our adherence to tradition and partly by recognizing when to transcend the elements of our tradition when former grounds of understanding are themselves transcended. In our humanness, we are loath to release long-held associations and values. Analogous to the long-held association and value of celibacy for the sacerdotal priesthood is the phenomenon of releasing the association and value of a loved one through death.

Earlier I asked why the bishops with whom I was in conversation were manifesting denial. Clearly, celibacy just goes with the territory. It is an association of value, fixed and firm, especially in the minds of those who have embraced it. It is so entrenched and has been made so sacrosanct that it is virtually a sin to question its obligatory nature. Perhaps an example of one of the vestiges of this "obligation" can serve to recognize a right that is being contravened by the continuance of the present discipline.

It will be recalled that I first thought about the ordained ministry when I was an adolescent. Although I did not respond by enrolling in the junior seminary at that age, many clerics alive today did exactly that. Since I have been in Seattle, it came to my attention that a priest who was struggling with his vocation disclosed to his congregation that he would be leaving the parish. He explained that he felt as though he was wearing two left shoes. One was very comfortable, but the other was pinching pretty bad and was very uncomfortable. Jan and I had occasion to be talking with another priest of our acquaintance whom we met while walking along the shore of Puget Sound. The priest who had announced his leaving to his assembly happened by, and the priest with us recognized him and called him over. He inquired of the priest's wellbeing and expressed fraternal concern. To his credit the leaving cleric shared that he was striving to find himself because, as he stated, "I have been doing this since I was fourteen."

I have thought about this many times since, and I am fortunate that I didn't leave home to go to the junior seminary at age fourteen. More importantly, I think of the injustice perpetrated in the life of the leaving cleric and how irretrievable that part of his life, should he now conclude that he ought to have married. For those having responsibility for the formation of individuals perceiving a call from God, this is serious business. Why do we encumber it so?

Psychological insights into the death and dying of human beings are analogous to the death and dying of **obligatory** celibacy in the church. Elizabeth Kübler-Ross's famous work *On Death and Dying* was published in 1969, four years after the end of the Second Vatican Council. In it she developed five stages of the dying process: (1) denial and isolation, (2) anger, (3) bargaining, (4) depression, and (5) acceptance.[4] We are seeing corresponding psychological human responses to the "dying" of obligatory celibacy. I have already given an example of the first stage of *denial*. I think denial is being manifested in a variety of ways throughout the church. In 1987 when my former spouse was dying, my pastor, Duncan MacDonell, responded to a comment of mine one day by saying, "Irene is ready, Ron, but you're not!"

For many years bishops have been trying to make tentative plans for the days when we have fewer priests. It always seemed to me that was "game playing." The archbishop of Seattle held a series of deanery meetings seeking ways to handle the coming crises. At one meeting I was impressed by the vibrant and energetic presentation of the archbishop. I then observed an elderly man stand to suggest to the archbishop that we consider ordaining married men to help us meet the need so eloquently illustrated. I was crushed to hear the archbishop berate the idea, and by implication the individual, because the celibate clergy had served us so well during our two thousand years of tradition. My response to this was *anger*, the second stage of psychological response to death and dying. I know that some priests have experienced anger as well. One such example is a priest who told me "they could have done something about this twenty years ago."

The new archbishop of Seattle has not yet taken up that planning game, but in January 2001 he strongly urged the faithful to pray for priestly vocations in his regular diocesan newspaper column. If we recall how we have been taught to pray as if everything depended upon God and act as though everything depended upon us, we may well view the urgings of both archbishops as "denial." This is in no way to be construed to mean prayer ought to be abandoned or that we should not have recourse to prayer. Indeed we ought always to act in hope and so I pray: "Hear, O God, my cry; listen to my prayer" (Ps 61).

Efforts have been initiated to close or amalgamate parishes because ***obligatory*** celibacy is dying. This is bargaining with the people of God if not with God. It gives me the same helpless feeling that had accompanied my "bargaining" with God for the life of Irene when she was dying in 1987. Could it be with the church as it was with me when Duncan said I wasn't ready? Yes, I believe so. The people of God, including priests, are ready but the Vatican bureaucracy and ruling hierarchy are not.

And there is a manifestation of *depression*. And yes, I do think a prayer of lament is in order, and so I pray:

> I am wearied with sighing;
> every night I flood my bed with weeping;
> I drench my couch with my tears,
> My eyes are dimmed with sorrow;
> They have aged because of all my foes. (Ps 6: 7–8).

Acceptance, the final stage of dying, will bring a resurrection to new life for the church. This will be true for individuals in the ordained ministry called to new growth as well as for the Body of Christ that will experience exceptional growth after centuries limited by patriarchal dominance.

Subsequent applications of Kübler-Ross's theory emphasize that these stages are not clear-cut, consecutive kinds of psychological responses. They occur somewhat elliptically, where the individual progresses to the next stage but then circles back to the former stage, vacillating as it were throughout the process. Advances in psychology, sociology, and anthropology have given much knowledge and awareness not available to church leaders in 1139. What in one age may have seemed wise in another age is folly. Despite this awareness, there are still leaders within the Catholic tradition who perpetuate the adolescent junior seminary model, knowing that the existing "law" will obligate such candidates to celibacy when they have "completed age twenty-five," the earliest age for priestly ordination according to canon 1031 §1. In justice, this practice ought to be discontinued. The minor seminary is a clearly proven failed system. Indeed it can be argued that the entire seminary system in the church is largely a failed system as explained in the preface of this book.

To further illustrate the anachronism of mandatory celibacy, I wish to bring the findings of Abraham Maslow to bear on the celibate tradition. Maslow, one of the great humanistic psychologists, developed the theory of human needs in the late 1960s, explaining these as hierarchical in nature. He believed that people are not merely controlled by mechanical forces but should be understood in terms of human potential. He set up a hierarchy with the basic physical needs placed at the bottom and the higher human needs at the top, as follows:

Self-Actualization Needs

The need for fulfillment: becoming devoted, wise, and creative, leading to the realization of one's full potential.

Esteem Needs

Need for a stable, firmly based high level of respect from self and others, to feel valuable.

Love, Affection, and Belongingness Needs

The need to escape loneliness and alienation, give and receive love, affection, and belonging.

Safety Needs

Felt by adults in emergencies and more frequently by children in their needs to be safe.

Physiological Needs

Biological needs, i.e., oxygen, food, water, warmth, protection from the elements.[5]

Looking at these starting from the bottom with the physiological needs, we realize that a child in school, for instance, isn't going to learn very much if he or she is hungry. These needs are the strongest because if deprived a person may die. In terms of safety needs, various occupations prompted by regulatory requirements now provide preventive equipment for employees such as hearing protection from occupational noise. Enforcement agencies authorize "backup" procedures and safety equipment for transporting prisoners in vehicles. Failing to meet safety needs can be injurious to the person. I remember a brother seminarian who had been a forester and required hearing aids in both ears, because the safety need for noise attenuation had not been adopted in his earlier career.

If we were to apply the behavioral scientist's hierarchy of needs to the Body of Christ, I suggest those needs would look something like this:

Spiritual Hierarchy of Needs of the People of God

Physiological: The spiritual needs are the "Bread of Life" and "Living Water," without which we would not survive.

Safety Needs: The needs are for the safe haven of community with leadership and harmony, to hear and express faith and thereby renew and deepen it. Deprivation results in victimization from loss, fear, or abuse that hinders the sanctification of our rising through the next levels of need.

Love, Affection, and Belonging: The need to become people of "The Way" living the precepts of love of God and neighbor. To the extent these needs are not met, frustration, loneliness, and even alienation occur.

Esteem Needs: The needs are for high levels of love of self and neighbor, to feel satisfied, self-confident, and valuable. Without these we feel weak, inferior, helpless, and even worthless.

Self-Actualization Needs: These needs are to achieve the highest levels of which we are capable, functioning fully in accord with the will of God. Failing to meet these needs results in restlessness and a feeling that we are lacking something.

Based upon the foregoing, I dare to illustrate what may happen to those in leadership positions, particularly the ordained within the Body of Christ, should their needs not be met:

Physiological: The "Bread of Life" and "Living Water" needs are largely met in First World countries, though not everywhere. For leaders adequate protection and rest from unrelenting demands and rejuvenation are vital. Some nonordained leaders are unable to participate in daily mass or communal liturgies because of scarce opportunities. Sometimes demands become overwhelming—too much for one person.

Safety: Personal discipline, leadership skills, and prayer buoyed by a support system, privacy, recreation, and time away from the office or workplace stresses are essential safety and security needs. Spiritual dryness, loss of confidence or interest, psychological breakdown can result if these needs are not met.

Love, Affection, and Belongingness Needs: Living at an established level of servanthood espousing the precepts of love modeled by Jesus underlies the needs of leaders in the Body of Christ. Firm discipline and spiritual practices are essential together with communication from family members, friends, and a support group, especially where a celibate lifestyle is being followed. These unfulfilled needs can render a person "at risk" in relation to someone who is vulnerable, may lead to addictive behavior, clandestine relationships, or abuse.

Esteem Needs: Affirmations from the local ordinary, his delegate, and other forms of recognition and achievement are critical needs for leaders in the Body of Christ. Having to be one of a crowd but not part of that crowd can produce feelings of inferiority, weakness, helplessness, or worthlessness.

Self-Actualization Needs: A high level of dedication, sensitivity, and resourcefulness associated with doing what they were born to do characterize the leader's needs at this level. Achieving this highest level of functioning may be elusive because of tradition, imposed lifestyle, careerism, or other expectations that treat one as being different or set apart. In certain environments institutional stresses can tend to promote mediocrity and this level simply cannot be met.

The challenge arising from my life story as presented herein is based on the overwhelming evidence that something is amiss in our perpetuation of obligatory celibacy. A celibate lifestyle accepted by an individual in response to a genuine call and gift from God as a personal choice is one thing. Continuing to make that choice of lifestyle obligatory across the board as a consequence of a calling from God to priesthood is a denial of the right of married men to respond to God's call to priesthood. It used to "go with the territory," but in my view and in the view of our greater awareness of human dignity developed through the Declaration on Religious Liberty, it ought not to be part of the territory any longer. Elimination of the forced and unnatural requirement of celibacy will be an emancipation greater by far than liberation from the Mosaic practice of circumcision in the infant church. It is striking how the words of St. Peter at the Council of Jerusalem apply to the present case.: "Why, then, are you now putting God to the test by placing on the shoulders of the disciples a yoke that neither our ancestors nor we have been able to bear? On the contrary, we believe that we are saved through the grace of the Lord Jesus, in the same way as they" (Acts 15:10–11). The yoke here was the requirement that gentile converts to Christianity undergo circumcision, but mandatory celibacy could apply just as well.

Like those candidates who accepted celibacy in order to honor their commitment to God, I too make this appeal with a generous heart, not knowing whether my aspirations toward ordained ministry have passed me by. In 1995, I attended the ordination of Father Dick Ward who was blessed with thirty-six years of marriage before his spouse entered into her new life in God. I had the privilege of sharing one seminary semester with Dick in Spokane. He is ten years my senior and his continued ministry as the pastor of a parish in the Archdiocese of Seattle is an inspiration.

Jan attended Dick's ordination with me, and while entering the church Jan encountered a nun who was her former colleague in ministry at Providence Medical Center. She commented to Jan, "I hope you won't have to die in order for Ron to be ordained someday!" When Jan told me of her comment, I received it as a great affirmation. I continue to wait and to be willing to serve. At the very least I pray that this writing will find favor with God and that its sharing influence will gain fruitful acceptance through the power of the Holy Spirit and expedite the further development of doctrine in the priesthood of Christ.

Having presented this work to influence the Catholic Church in a move toward truth and justice, I know that many concerns will arise when the right of clergy to marry is restored. Many decisions will have to be made. I optimistically present some suggestions for consideration:

1. Bypass the enclosed seminary system for married candidates by expanding the already successful model for preparing married deacons.
2. Authorize the diocesan bishop to ordain whomever he in conjunction with his people want.
3. Ordain to priesthood suitable married deacons who have a genuine priestly vocation.
4. Invite back into active ministry those already ordained men who have married and wish to be reconciled and who otherwise have remained faithful and want to resume priestly ministry.
5. Carefully select and prepare good married candidates:
   a. who have been married for many years or whose children are independent or at least away to college;
   b. whose wives are enthusiastic, supportive, and willing to share the preparation as deacons' wives have done;
   c. who have enthusiastic recommendations from pastors and Catholics who know them well.
6. Ordain several such "couples" in small parishes, e.g., small rural parishes, to prevent burnout, and a dozen or so in large parishes, so they may relieve each other and be able to take three months off annually to visit children, grandchildren, and rest up, to ensure that priesthood will not interfere with their family responsibilities.
7. Identify clear and open expectations with relevant job descriptions for bishops and pastors.
8. Establish corresponding means for regular evaluations that will

eliminate the practice of unquestioned autonomy in favor of true collegiality in the body of Christ.

Our church tribunals have made great strides in learning about our humanness. I am not suggesting the change to a married clergy will be without problems, but I trust that the problems that do arise will be less traumatic than those we have experienced, because the change will accord more closely with the design of God. We can learn much from the married clergy in other Christian churches. It is time for the people of God to shoulder their responsibility for the mission of Jesus and to take a stand. Let us begin.

ACKNOWLEDGMENTS

The research for this writing began in 1991 but my story that is integrated with the research began long before. Consequently I am indebted to countless people that made this possible. My thanks to each of you as I attempt to name the significant, knowing I will miss the important. So here I go!

Special thanks to Agnes and Frank who gave me life, to my brothers Bernie, Chuck, Bill, and Bob who share in my life, posthumously to Irene my friend and confidant who gave me love, much strength, and five wonderful children. I thank Eugene, Michael, Veronica, Monica, and John, their spouses and my grandchildren for their love and support, despite my leaving. I thank my in-laws, Ruby and the late Louis Hebert, my stepsons Frank, Tim, and Deacon Donald, their spouses, and my step-grandchildren for their love and acceptance of me.

I am grateful for the prayers and support of my godparents and my special friends Joe and Rita Deck and Bill Grant, and for the guidance and ministry of so many good priests and religious: especially Eugene Violini, Bill White, Albert Laisnez, Karl Rabb, Bernadette O'Neil, Duncan MacDonnell, Archbishop Joseph MacNeil, Armand Nigro, Charles Skok, John Heagle, Fran Ferder, and George Maloney. In a particular way I thank John Zeder, Bishop Skylstad, Thomas Quinn, Joseph Doogan, and Kevin Moran.

In the ten years that I have been in Seattle I became acquainted with many wonderful people in St. Bernadette parish and Our Lady of Fatima parish who helped me to grow in my faith and love of God. It is impossible to name everybody but Bob Brolan representing many, especially the morning group, looms large in my memory and gratitude, as does Don Zeek for his faith, generosity, and computer skills.

I am enormously grateful to Frank Oveis, my editor, for finding value in my writing and for his sensitivity and patient questioning that helped to keep me on track.

Lastly I thank my wife Janice for putting up with my impatience and the tedium associated with this writing. Most of all I thank her for leading me closer to God, for sharing her baptismal priesthood, and for confirming to me and countless others that women are indeed called to the ordained ministry in the Catholic Church. Without her love and support this book would not have been possible.

BIBLIOGRAPHY

Basset, William, and Peter Huizing, eds. *Celibacy in the Church*. New York: Herder and Herder, 1972.
Berry, Jason. *Lead Us Not into Temptation: Catholic Priests and the Sexual Abuse of Children*. Chicago: University of Illinois Press, 2000.
Blenkinsopp, Joseph. *Celibacy, Ministry, Church*. New York: Herder and Herder, 1968.
Bradshaw, John. *Bradshaw on the Family: A Revolutionary Way of Self-Discovery*. Deerfield Beach, Fla.: Health Communications, 1988
Brown, Peter. *The Body and Society: Men, Women and Sexual Renunciation in Early Christianity*. New York: Columbia University Press, 1988.
Byrne, Lavinia, IVBM. *Woman at the Altar: The Ordination of Women in the Roman Catholic Church*. London: Mowbray, A Cassell Imprint, 1994; Collegeville, Minn.: Liturgical Press. New York: Continuum, 1998.
Catechism of the Catholic Church. Second Edition. Washington, D.C.: United States Catholic Conference, 1997.
Cece, Joe. "Celibacy Is Not the Issue." catholicism.guide@miningco.com. February 15, 1998.
Cochini, Christian, S.J. *Apostolic Origins of Priestly Celibacy*. San Francisco: Ignatius Press, 1990.
Code of Canon Law: Latin-English Edition. Washington, D.C.: Canon Law Society, 1983.
Collins, Mary, O.S.B. *Two Theologies of Eucharist*. Videocassette Tape 1, Presentation to the General Chapter of St. Scholastica. Benetvision 355. Erie, Penn., 1998.
Congar, Yves, O.P. *A Gospel Priesthood*. Trans. P.F. Hepburne-Scott. New York: Herder and Herder, 1967.
Coriden, James A., et al. *The Code of Canon Law: A Text and Commentary*. Study Edition. New York: Paulist Press, 1985.
Cozzens, Donald B. *The Spirituality of the Diocesan Priest*. Collegeville, Minn.: Liturgical Press, 1997.

———. *The Changing Face of the Priesthood: A Reflection on the Priest's Crisis of Soul.* Collegeville, Minn.: Liturgical Press, 2000.

Eagan, Joseph F., S.J. *Restoration and Renewal: The Church in the Third Millennium.* Kansas City, Mo.: Sheed & Ward, 1995.

Flannery, Austin O.P. *Vatican Council II. Volume 1: The Conciliar and Post Conciliar Documents.* Northport, N.Y.: Costello, 1975 and 1984.

———. *Vatican Council II. Volume 2: More Post Conciliar Documents.* Collegeville, Minn.: Liturgical Press, 1982.

Freire, Paulo. *Pedagogy of the Oppressed.* Trans. Myra B. Ramos. New York: Continuum, 1990.

Genovesi, Vincent J., S.J. *In Pursuit of Love: Catholic Morality and Human Sexuality.* Wilmington, Del.: Michael Glazier, 1987.

Gonsalves, Milton A. *Fagothey's Right and Reason: Ethics in Theory and Practice.* Ninth Edition. Columbus: Merrill Publishing, 1989.

Häring, Bernard, C.S.S.R. *Priesthood Imperiled: A Critical Examination of Ministry in the Catholic Church.* Liguori, Mo.: Triumph Books, 1996.

John Paul II. *Fides et Ratio* [Faith and Reason] Papal Encyclical. Rome, September 14, 1998.

Kennedy, Eugene. *Tomorrow's Catholics, Yesterday's Church: The Two Cultures of American Catholicism.* Liguori, Mo.: Triumph Books, 1988.

———. *The Unhealed Wound: The Church and Human Sexuality.* New York: St. Martin's Press, 2001.

Kübler-Ross, Elisabeth, *On Death and Dying.* New York: MacMillan Publishing, 1969.

Liebert, Elizabeth, SNJM. *Changing Life Patterns: Adult Development in Spiritual Direction.* St. Louis, Mo.: Chalice Press, 2000.

Maslow, Abraham. "Hierarchy of Needs." http://www.connect.net/georgen/maslow.htm

McBrien, Richard. "Another Scandal." *The Catholic Northwest Progress,* April 19, 2001: 6.

McKenzie, John L., S.J. *Dictionary of the Bible.* New York: MacMillan Publishing, 1965.

Meeks, Wayne A. *The First Urban Christians: The Social World of the Apostle Paul.* New Haven: Yale University Press, 1983.

Murphy, Thomas J. *Pastoral Care of Parish Communities.* Archdiocese of Seattle, 1994.

O'Meara, Thomas F., O.P. *Theology of Ministry,* Completely Revised Edition. New York: Paulist Press, 1999.

Radcliffe, Timothy, O.P. "Leaving Behind the Usual Signs of Identity." *Origins,* August 1996.

Ranke-Heineman, Uta. *Eunuchs for the Kingdom of Heaven: Women, Sexuality and the Catholic Church.* Trans. Peter Heinegg. New York: Doubleday, 1990.

Rathus, Spencer A., et al. Human Sexuality in a World of Diversity. 4th Edition. Boston: Allyn and Bacon, 2000.

Schafe, Anne Wilson, and Diane Fassel. *The Addictive Organization.* New York: Harper & Row, 1988.

Schillebeeckx, Edward, O.P. *Celibacy.* Trans. C.A.L. Jarrott. New York: Sheed and Ward, 1968.

———. *The Church with a Human Face: A New and Expanded Theology of Ministry.* New York: Crossroad, 1988.

Shannon, William H. "With You I Am a Christian." *America,* June 5–12, 1999: 12–13.

Smith, Karen Sue. *Priesthood in the Modern World: A Reader.* Franklin, Wis.: Sheed & Ward, 1999.

Steinfels, Peter. "The Church's Sex Abuse Crisis." *Commonweal,* April 19, 2002: 19.

Stickler, Alfons Maria Cardinal. *The Case for Clerical Celibacy: Its Historical Development and Theological Foundations.* Trans. Brian Ferme. San Francisco: Ignatius Press, 1995.

Tanner, Norman P., S.J., ed. *Decrees of the Ecumenical Councils, Volume 1: Nicaea I to Lateran V.* Washington D.C.: Georgetown University Press, 1990.

Unsworth, Tim. "Church Labors under Heavy Hierarchy." *National Catholic Reporter,* July 14, 2000: 19.

Wicks, Robert J., Richard D. Parsons, and Donald Capps, eds. *Clinical Handbook of Pastoral Counseling.* New York: Paulist Press, 1985.

Wills, Garry. *Papal Sin: Structures of Deceit.* New York: Doubleday, 2000.

Winter, Gordon. Chair. Commission of Enquiry into Sexual Abuse of Children. Archdiocese of Newfoundland, 1990

Winter, Miriam Therese. *Out of the Depths: The Story of Ludmila Javorova Ordained Roman Catholic Priest.* New York: Crossroad, 2001.

Wintz, Jack, O.F.M. "The Child Sex Abuse Scandal," *Friar Jack's E-Spirations American Catholic.org* 4-8-02.

NOTES

Introduction

1. John L. McKenzie, *Dictionary of the Bible*, p. 813.
2. Pope John Paul II, *Fides et Ratio*, p. 3.

Chapter 2: Before Celibacy Was Obligatory

1. Joseph Blenkisopp, *Celibacy, Ministry, Church*, pp. 21–24.
2. Spencer A. Rathus et al., *Human Sexuality in a World of Diversity*, pp. 12–14.
3. Peter Brown, *The Body and Society*, pp. 6–7.
4. Ibid., pp. 10–12.
5. Wayne A. Meeks, *The First Urban Christians*, p. 23.
6. Brown, *The Body and Society*, pp. 8–9.
7. Edward Schillebeeckx, *Celibacy*, pp. 26–28.
8. Brown, *The Body and Society*, pp. 140–41.
9. Ibid., pp. 204–5.
10. Yves Congar, *A Gospel Priesthood*, pp. 74–85.
11. Ibid., pp. 85–87.
12. Schillebeeckx, *Celibacy*, p. 29.
13. Brown, *The Body and Society*, pp. 142–44.
14. Edward Schillebeeckx, *The Church with a Human Face*, pp. 240–43.
15. Brown, *The Body and Society*, pp. 202–5.
16. Ibid., pp. 67–68.
17. Alfons Maria Cardinal Stickler, *The Case for Clerical Celibacy*, pp. 21–23.
18. Blenkinsopp, *Celibacy, Ministry, Church*, pp. 20–21.
19. Stickler, *The Case for Clerical Celibacy*, pp. 17–18.
20. Schillebeeckx, *Celibacy*, pp. 29–44.

21. Christian Cochini, *Apostolic Origins of Priestly Celibacy*, pp.8–9.
22. Brown, *The Body and Society*, pp. 348–51.
23. Cochini, *Apostolic Origins of Celibacy*, pp. 4–5.
24. Schillebeeckx, *The Church with a Human Face*, pp. 240–43.
25. Brown, *The Body and Society*, pp. 292–93.
26. Ibid., pp. 396–426.
27. Brown, *The Body and Society*, pp. 409–12.
28. Austin Flannery, *Vatican Council II*, 1:5.

Chapter 4: Celibacy Becomes Mandatory for Ordination

1 Edward Schillebeeckx, *The Church with a Human Face*, p. 240.
2. Norman B. Tanner, ed. *Decrees of the Ecumenical Councils*, 1:191.
3. Ibid., p. 193.
4. Ibid., p. 198.
5. Schillebeeckx, *The Church with a Human Face*, p. 243.
6. Joseph Blenkinsopp, *Celibacy, Ministry, Church*, pp. 22–35.
7 Schillebeeckx, *The Church with a Human Face*, p. 244.
8. William Basset and Peter Huizing, eds., *Celibacy in the Church*, pp. 57–59.
9. Ibid., pp. 59–61.
10. Ibid., pp. 62–66.
11. Ibid., pp. 69–71.
12. Ibid., pp. 72–74.

Chapter 6: The Priesthood That I Knew

1. Donald B. Cozzens, *The Spirituality of the Diocesan Priest*, p. 50.
2. Joseph F. Eagan, *Restoration and Renewal*, pp. 32 and 156.

Chapter 8: Official Changes Made to the Priesthood

1. Austin Flannery, *Vatican Council II*, 1:892.
2. Ibid., 2:290.
3. Ibid., 1:427–32.
4. Ibid., 2:186.
5. Ibid., 1:350–426.
6. Ibid., 1:1–40.
7. Ibid., 1:766–98.
8. Karen Sue Smith, ed., *Priesthood in the Modern World*, p. viii.

Chapter 10: The Ordained Priesthood in Crisis

1. William Bassett and Peter Huizing, eds., *Celibacy in the Church*, p. 136.
2. Uta Ranke-Heinemann, *Eunuchs for the Kingdom of Heaven*, p. 118.
3. Gordon Winter, *Commission of Enquiry into Sexual Abuse of Children*, p. 87.
4. Ibid., p. 97.
5. Ibid., p. 161.

6. Jason Berry, *Lead Us Not into Temptation*, pp. 365–66.
7. Eugene Kennedy, *The Unhealed Wound*, p. 10.
8. Berry, *Lead Us Not into Temptation*, p. 75.
9. Garry Wills, *Papal Sin*, p. 175.
10. Ibid., p. 184.
11. Ibid., p. 185.
12. Ibid., pp. 185–86.
13. Austin Flannery, *Vatican Council II*, 1:806.
14. Winter, *Commission of Enquiry into Sexual Abuse of Children*, pp. 87 and 97.
15. Kennedy, *The Unhealed Wound*, pp. 15–16.
16. Elizabeth Liebert, *Changing Life Patterns*, pp. 18–19.
17. Kennedy, *The Unhealed Wound*, p. 123.
18. Berry, *Lead Us Not into Temptation*, pp. 173–74.
19. Donald B. Cozzens, *The Changing Face of the Priesthood*, p. 100.
20. Berry, *Lead Us Not into Temptation*, p. 216.
21. Joseph F. Eagan, *Restoration and Renewal*, pp. 13–14.
22. Flannery, *Vatican Council II*, 1:370.
23. Berry, *Lead Us Not into Temptation*, p. xxii.
24. Peter Steinfels, "The Church's Sex Abuse Scandal," *Commonweal*, April 19, 2000:19.
25. Kennedy, *The Unhealed Wound*, p. 136.
26. Jack Wintz, "The Child Sex Abuse Scandal," *Friar Jack's E-Spirations*, americancatholic.org 4-8-02.
27. Richard McBrien, "Another Scandal," *The Catholic Northwest Progress*, April 19, 2001:6.
28. Ibid., p. 6.
29. James A. Corriden et al., *The Code of Canon Law*, canon 1037.
30. Berry, *Lead Us Not into Temptation*, p. xxii.
31. Bernard Häring, *Priesthood Imperiled*, p. 133.
32. Wills, *Papal Sin*, pp. 155–56.
33. Kennedy, *The Unhealed Wound*, p. 133.
34. William H. Shannon, "With You I Am a Christian," *America*, June 5, 1999:12–13.
35. Coriden et al., *The Code of Canon Law*, p. 728.
36. Ibid., pp. 147–48.
37. Ibid., pp. 723–24.
38. Ibid., pp. 731 and 209.
39. *Catechism of the Catholic Church*, p. 535.
40. Lavinia Byrne, *Woman at the Altar*, p. 96.
41. Paulo Freire, *Pedagogy of the Oppressed*, pp. 27–33.

Chapter 11: My Call to Priesthood

1. Vincent J. Genovesi, S.J., *In Pursuit of Love: Catholic Morality and Human Sexuality*, p. 27.

Chapter 12: Contemporary Priesthood

1. Thomas F. O'Meara, *Theology of Ministry*, p. 8.
2. James A. Coriden et al., *The Code of Canon Law*, pp. 143–44.
3. Ibid., p. 717.
4. Joseph F. Eagan, *Restoration and Renewal*, p. 29.

5. Donald B. Cozzens, *The Spirituality of the Diocesan Priest*, p. 51.
6. Ibid., p.151.
7. Coriden, *The Code of Canon Law*, p. 143.
8. Timothy Rdacliffe, O.P., Master of the Dominicans spoke on this topic at the Conference of Major Superiors of Men in 1996. See his "Leaving Behind the Usual Signs of Identity," *Origins*, August 1996.
9. Coriden, *The Code of Canon Law*, pp. 167–68.
10. O'Meara, *Theology of Ministry*, p. 19.
11. Eugene Kennedy, *Tomorrow's Catholics Yesterday's Church*, pp. xi-xiv.
12. Mary Collins, *Two Theologies of Eucharist*, Videocassette Tape 1.
13. Ibid.
14. O'Meara, *Theology of Ministry*, pp. 17–18.
15. Ibid., p. 18.
16. Tim Unsworth, "Church Labors under Heavy Hierarchy," *National Catholic Reporter*, July 14:2000:19.

Chapter 13: On the Right Track

1. Robert J. Wicks et al., eds. *Clinical Handbook of Pastoral Counseling*, pp. 452–72.
2. John Bradshaw, *Bradshaw on the Family*, p. 22.
3. Milton A. Gonsalves, *Fagothey's Right and Reason*, pp. 140–47.
4. Austin Flannery, *Vatican Council II*, 1:801.
5. Thomas J. Murphy, *Pastoral Care of Parish Communities*, p. 6.

Chapter 14: The Call Questioned

1. Edward Schillebeeckx, *The Church with a Human Face*, p. 242.
2. Austin Flannery, *Vatican Council II*, 1:707–24.
3. Ibid., 1:863–902.
4. Ibid., 1:7:15–16.
5. James Coriden et al., *The Code of Canon Law*, p. 210.
6. Ibid.
7. Miriam Therese Winter, *Out of the Depths*, p. 211.
8. Joseph F. Eagan, *Restoration and Renewal*, p. 35.
9. Schillebeeckx, *Celibacy*, pp. 25–53.
10. Eagan, *Restoration and Renewal*, p. 36.
11. Joe Cece, "Celibacy Is Not the Issue," catholicism.guide@miningco.com
12. Eagan, *Restoration and Renewal*, p. 13.
13. Garry Wills, *Papal Sin*, pp. 122–23.
14. Eagan, *Restoration and Renewal*, pp. 183–85.

Chapter 15: A Sequel

1. Edward Schillebeeckx, *The Church with a Human Face*, pp. 209–10.
2. John Bradshaw, *Bradshaw on the Family*, p. 22.
3. Ann Wilson Schafe, *The Addictive Organization*, pp. 26 and 109.
4. Elisabeth Kübler-Ross, *On Death and Dying*, pp. 38–137.
5. Abraham Maslow, "Hierarchy of Needs," http://www.connect.net/georgen/maslow.htm